OCR A Level Biology A Lab Book

Published by Pearson Education Limited, 80 Strand, London, WC2R 0RL.

www.pearsonschoolsandfecolleges.co.uk

Text © Pearson Education Limited 2017
Typeset and illustrated by Tech-Set Ltd Gateshead
Original illustrations © Pearson Education Limited 2015
Cover design by Pete Stratton
Cover photo/illustration © Fotolia: nobeastsofierce

First published 2017

19 18 17 16
10 9 8 7 6 5 4 3 2 1

British Library Cataloguing in Publication Data
A catalogue record for this book is available from the British Library

ISBN 978 1 292 20026 2

Copyright notice
All rights reserved. No part of this publication may be reproduced in any form or by any means (including photocopying or storing it in any medium by electronic means and whether or not transiently or incidentally to some other use of this publication) without the written permission of the copyright owner, except in accordance with the provisions of the Copyright, Designs and Patents Act 1988 or under the terms of a licence issued by the Copyright Licensing Agency, Barnards Inn, 86 Fetter Lane, London EC4A 1EN(www.cla.co.uk). Applications for the copyright owner's written permission should be addressed to the publisher.

Printed in Italy by Lego S.p.A

Acknowledgements
The publishers would like to thank Gillian Lindsey for her contributions to the text.

The publishers would also like to thank Michael Boyle, Robert Duncan and Wade Nottingham for their work on the original Teacher Resource Pack.

Note from the publisher
Pearson has robust editorial processes, including answer and fact checks, to ensure the accuracy of the content in this publication, and every effort is made to ensure this publication is free of errors. We are, however, only human, and occasionally errors do occur. Pearson is not liable for any misunderstandings that arise as a result of errors in this publication, but it is our priority to ensure that the content is accurate. If you spot an error, please do contact us at resourcescorrections@pearson.com so we can make sure it is corrected.

1 Using paper chromatography to separate a mixture of amino acids
2 Serial dilutions
3 Qualitative testing of a reducing sugar
4 Determining glucose concentration
5 Effect of substrate concentration on catalase activity
6 Investigating the effect of pH on catalase activity
7 Investigating the effect of temperature on amylase activity
8 Investigating the effect of temperature on membrane permeability
9 Finding the water potential of onion tissue
10 Observing stages in mitosis
11 Effect of surface area:volume ratio on diffusion rate
12 Using a spirometer to make measurements
13 Dissecting the heart
14 Using a potometer to determine water uptake
15 Quantitative analysis of the distribution of species in a habitat
16 Observe and make annotated diagrams of the pancreas
17 Observe and make annotated diagrams of the kidney
18 Observe and make annotated diagrams of skeletal muscle
19 Use a biosensor to investigate glucose concentration in mock urine
20 Investigate immobilised pectinase
21 Investigate immobilised lipase
22 Investigate the effect of antibacterial agents on bacterial growth
23 Compare anaerobic and aerobic respiration
24 Investigate the effect of substrate type on yeast respiration
25 Investigate the effect of carbon dioxide on the rate of photosynthesis
26 Investigate the effect of changing light intensity on the photosynthesis rate of *Cabomba*
27 Investigate reaction times, nerve transmission and multiple sclerosis
28 Investigate succession in a sand dune using a line transect
29 DNA gel electrophoresis
30 Observe the effect of ATP on muscle contraction

Practical activity group (PAG)	Techniques/skills covered (minimum)	Covered
1 Microscopy	• use of a light microscope at high power and low power, use of a graticule, 1.2.2 (d) • production of scientific drawings from observations with annotations, 1.2.2 (e)	☐ ☐
2 Dissection	• safe use of instruments for dissection of an animal or plant organ, 1.2.2(j) • use of a light microscope at high power and low power, use of a graticule, 1.2.2 (d) • production of scientific drawings from observations with annotations, 1.2.2 (e)	☐ ☐ ☐
3 Sampling techniques	• use of sampling techniques in fieldwork, 1.2.2 (k) • production of scientific drawings from observations with annotations, 1.2.2 (e)	☐ ☐
4 Rates of enzyme controlled reactions	• use of appropriate apparatus to record a range of quantitative measurements (to include mass, time, volume, temperature, length and pH), 1.2.2 (a) • use of laboratory glassware apparatus for a variety of experimental techniques to include serial dilutions, 1.2.2 (c) • use of ICT such as computer modelling, or data logger to collect data, or use of software to process data, 1.2.2 (l)	☐ ☐ ☐
5 Colorimeter OR potometer	• use of appropriate apparatus to record quantitative measurements, such as a colorimeter or potometer, 1.2.2 (b) • use of laboratory glassware apparatus for a variety of experimental techniques to include serial dilutions, 1.2.2 (c)	☐ ☐
6 Chromatography OR electrophoresis	• separation of biological compounds using thin layer/paper chromatography or electrophoresis, 1.2.2 (g)	☐
7 Microbiological techniques	• use of laboratory glassware apparatus for a variety of experimental techniques to include serial dilutions, 1.2.2 (c) • use of microbiological aseptic techniques, including the use of agar plates and broth, 1.2.2 (i)	☐ ☐
8 Transport in and out of cells	• use of appropriate apparatus to record a range of quantitative measurements (to include mass, time, volume, temperature, length and pH), 1.2.2 (a) • use of laboratory glassware apparatus for a variety of experimental techniques to include serial dilutions, 1.2.2 (c) • use of ICT such as computer modelling, or data logger to collect data, or use of software to process data, 1.2.2 (l)	☐ ☐ ☐
9 Qualitative testing	• use of laboratory glassware apparatus for a variety of experimental techniques to include serial dilutions, 1.2.2 (c) • use of qualitative reagents to identify biological molecules, 1.2.2 (f)	☐ ☐
10 Investigation using a data logger OR computer modelling	• use of ICT such as computer modelling, or data logger to collect data, or use of software to process data, 1.2.2 (l) • apply investigative approaches, 1.2.1 (a)	☐ ☐
11 Investigation into the measurement of plant or animal responses	• safe and ethical use of organisms to measure plant or animal responses and physiological functions, 1.2.2 (h) • apply investigative approaches, 1.2.1 (a)	☐ ☐
12 Research skills	• apply investigative approaches, 1.2.1 (a) • use online and offline research skills, 1.2.1 (h) • correctly cite sources of information, 1.2.1 (i)	☐ ☐ ☐

There is no practical endorsement (direct assessment of practical skills) for AS qualifications. However, students must be able to answer questions relating to practical work in the written papers at both AS and A level.

For A level students, assessment of practical skills can be carried out throughout the two-year course. In this Lab Book, practicals 1 to 15 cover first year work, while practicals 16 to 30 cover second year content. This book has practical activities across all the Practical Activity Groups (PAGs) in the specification. Some PAGs, however, lie within the content of the second year of the course.

In order to achieve a **pass** for the Practical Endorsement at A level, students will need to have completed a minimum of 12 practical activities from the Practical Activity Groups (PAGs) and to have met the expectations of the Common Practical Assessment Criteria (CPAC). Students will be expected to develop these competencies through the acquisition of the technical skills demonstrated in any practical activity undertaken throughout the course of study. The practical activities will provide opportunities for demonstrating competence in the skills identified, together with the use of apparatus and practical techniques.

Students may work in groups but must be able to demonstrate and record independent evidence of their competency. This must include evidence of independent application of investigative approaches and methods to practical work. Teachers who award a pass to their students need to be confident that the student consistently and routinely exhibits the competencies listed below before completion of the A level course.

While the Publishers have made every attempt to ensure that advice on the qualification and its assessment is accurate, the official specification and associated assessment guidance materials are the only authoritative source of information and should always be referred to for definitive guidance.

CPAC statements

1 Follows written procedures	**a)** Correctly follows instructions to carry out the experimental techniques or procedures.
2 Applies investigative approaches and methods when using instruments and equipment	**a)** Correctly uses appropriate instrumentation, apparatus and materials (including ICT) to carry out investigative activities, experimental techniques and procedures with minimal assistance or prompting. **b)** Carries out techniques or procedures methodically, in sequence and in combination, identifying practical issues and making adjustments when necessary. **c)** Identifies and controls significant quantitative variables where applicable, and plans approaches to take account of variables that cannot readily be controlled. **d)** Selects appropriate equipment and measurement strategies in order to ensure suitably accurate results.
3 Safely uses a range of practical equipment and materials	**a)** Identifies hazards and assesses risks associated with these hazards, making safety adjustments as necessary, when carrying out experimental techniques and procedures in the lab or field. **b)** Uses appropriate safety equipment and approaches to minimise risks with minimal prompting.
4 Makes and records observations	**a)** Makes accurate observations relevant to the experimental or investigative procedure. **b)** Obtains accurate, precise and sufficient data for experimental and investigative procedures and records this methodically using appropriate units and conventions.
5 Researches, references and reports	**a)** Uses appropriate software and/or tools to process data, carry out research and report findings. **b)** Sources of information are cited demonstrating that research has taken place, supporting planning and conclusions.

Practical	Date	CPAC statements											Evidence/comment
		1a	2a	2b	2c	2d	3a	3b	4a	4b	5a	5b	
1 Using paper chromatography to separate a mixture of amino acids													
2 Serial dilutions													
3 Qualitative testing of a reducing sugar													
4 Determining glucose concentration													
5 Effect of substrate concentration on catalase activity													
6 Investigating the effect of pH on catalase activity													
7 Investigating the effect of temperature on amylase activity													
8 Investigating the effect of temperature on membrane permeability													
9 Finding the water potential of onion tissue													
10 Observing stages in mitosis													
11 Effect of surface area: volume ratio on diffusion rate													
12 Using a spirometer to make measurements													
13 Dissecting the heart													
14 Using a potometer to determine water uptake													
15 Quantitative analysis of the distribution of species in a habitat													

Key: W – Working towards Y – Criteria met N – Criteria not met A – Absent

Practical	Date	CPAC statements											Evidence/comment
		1a	2a	2b	2c	2d	3a	3b	4a	4b	5a	5b	
16 Observe and make annotated diagrams of the pancreas													
17 Observe and make annotated diagrams of the kidney													
18 Observe and make annotated diagrams of skeletal muscle													
19 Use a biosensor to investigate glucose concentration in mock urine													
20 Investigate immobilised pectinase													
21 Investigate immobilised lipase													
22 Investigate the effect of antibacterial agents on bacterial growth													
23 Compare anaerobic and aerobic respiration													
24 Investigate the effect of substrate type on yeast respiration													
25 Investigate the effect of carbon dioxide on the rate of photosynthesis													
26 Investigate the effect of changing light intensity on the photosynthesis rate of *Cabomba*													
27 Investigate reaction times, nerve transmission and multiple sclerosis													
28 Investigate succession in a sand dune using a line transect													
29 DNA gel electrophoresis													
30 Observe the effect of ATP on muscle contraction													

Key: W – Working towards Y – Criteria met N – Criteria not met A – Absent

Practical 1
Using paper chromatography to separate a mixture of amino acids

PAG 6

CPAC links		Evidence	Done
1a	Correctly follows instructions to carry out the experimental techniques or procedures.	Practical procedure	
2d	Selects appropriate equipment and measurement strategies in order to ensure suitably accurate results.	Practical procedure	
3b	Uses appropriate safety equipment and approaches to minimise risks with minimal prompting.	Practical procedure	
4a	Makes accurate observations relevant to the experimental or investigative procedure.	Measurements and answers to questions	

Diagram

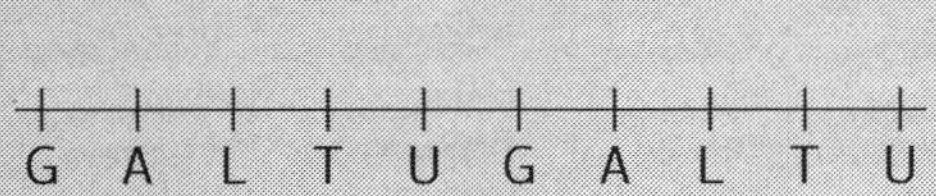

Figure A. Labelling of the origin

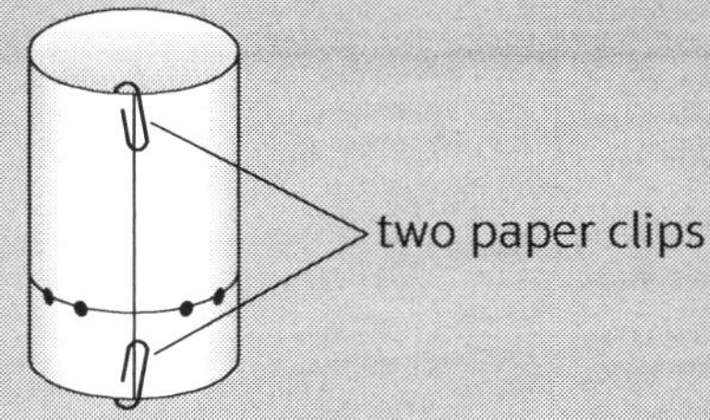

Figure B. Rolling the paper into a cylinder

Procedure

1. Pour 30 cm^3 of the solvent into a 500 cm^3 beaker and cover the beaker tightly with a piece of aluminium foil. You may need to mix the solvent yourself; in this case, mix 10 cm^3 of ammonia solution with 20 cm^3 of propan-2-ol.
2. Using a ruler and pencil, draw a faint line (the origin) about 1.5 cm from the bottom edge of the chromatography paper.
3. Along the origin, mark 10 light dots at intervals of approximately 2 cm. Label the dots as shown in Figure A. G, A, L and T correspond with the four known amino acids; U corresponds with the unknown mixture of amino acids.
4. Using capillary tubes, place some of each solution on the appropriate dots on the pencil line. Use a different capillary tube for each solution. Each spot on the paper should be no larger than 3 mm in diameter. Allow the spots to dry and then repeat.
5. Roll the paper to form a cylinder. Clip the ends together with a pair of paper clips (one at the top and one at the bottom as shown in Figure B). Make sure the edges of the paper do not touch. You can use staples instead of paper clips, if advised by your teacher.
6. Place the paper in a drying oven at approximately 100 °C for a few minutes, until fully dry.
7. Lower the paper into the beaker of solvent, making sure it does not touch the sides of the beaker. Ensure that the surface of the solvent is below the pencil line. Cover the beaker tightly with the aluminium foil.

Objectives

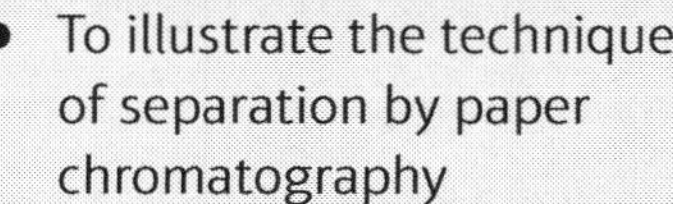

- To illustrate the technique of separation by paper chromatography
- To separate different amino acids
- To identify amino acids from R_f values

Equipment

- eye protection
- disposable gloves
- solvent (ammonia solution and propan-2-ol)
- ninhydrin spray
- glycine solution
- aspartic acid solution
- leucine solution
- tyrosine solution
- an 'unknown' solution containing one or two of the above amino acids
- aluminium foil
- paper clips and/or staples
- pencil
- ruler
- capillary tube
- chromatography paper
- 500 cm^3 beaker
- oven

Safety

- Eye protection and disposable gloves must be worn.
- Propan-2-ol is flammable. Keep away from naked flames.
- Ninhydrin spray is an irritant and flammable. Keep away from naked flames.
- Only use ninhydrin spray in a fume cupboard.
- Do not let ninhydrin spray, ammonia solution or hydrochloric acid come into contact with skin or eyes.

Irritant

Corrosive

Flammable

8 Leave the paper in the beaker with the solvent for 1–2 hours. After this, take out the paper and use a pencil to mark where the solvent has reached (the solvent front). Then set the paper upside down to dry.

9 Once the solvent has evaporated, remove the paper clips or staples and open the cylinder. Hang the paper in a fume cupboard.

10 In the fume cupboard, spray the paper lightly, but evenly, with ninhydrin and leave it to dry.

11 Place the paper in an oven at 100–110 °C for around 10 minutes, until all the spots have developed.

12 Draw around the spots and measure and record the distance travelled by each spot from the origin line. (Measure from the origin to the centre of each spot.) Also measure the distance the solvent travelled (the solvent front).

Chromatogram (Use this space to stick in your chromatogram.)

Record your results and calculations here.

Learning tips

- Amino acids differ in the structure of their R group. This affects properties such as solubility and bonding.
- Remember that R_f values simply describe a ratio of the distance travelled by a substance compared to the solvent front. If a substance travelled half the distance of the solvent front, its R_f value would be 0.5. As they are ratios, R_f values are written without units.

Analysis of results

- Calculate the R_f value for each spot. Use the formula:

$$R_f = \frac{\text{distance moved by spot}}{\text{distance moved by solvent front}}$$

  Make your calculations and record your results in the space above.
- Determine the composition of the unknown amino acid by visual comparison of the spot colours and by comparison of the R_f values.

Questions

1 How variable were the class results? Suggest reasons for any variation.

2 Why do amino acids move at different rates up the chromatography paper?

3 Which property of amino acids is responsible for this?

4 Your R_f values are unlikely to agree exactly with published values. Why might this be?

PAG 5 | 9

CPAC links		Evidence	Done
1a	Correctly follows instructions to carry out the experimental techniques or procedures.	Practical procedure	
2d	Selects appropriate equipment and measurement strategies in order to ensure suitably accurate results.	Practical procedure	

Objective

- To make a serial dilution

Equipment

- 10% glucose solution
- six test tubes
- labels or a grease pencil/OHP pen
- test tube rack
- distilled water
- five 1 cm³ graduated pipettes
- pipette filler
- 10 cm³ graduated pipette

Diagram

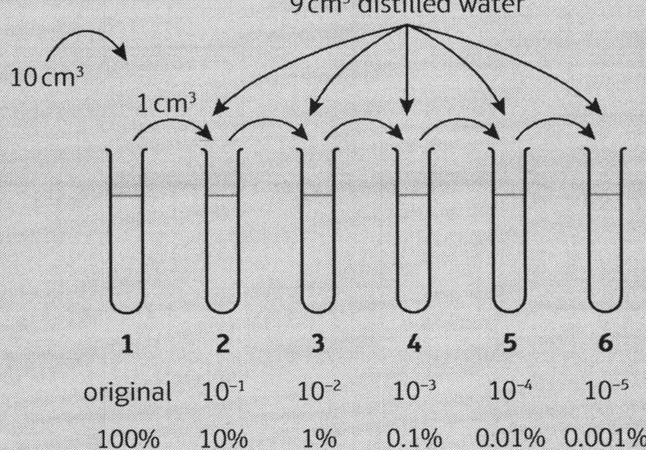

Figure A. Serial dilutions

Procedure

1. Label the six test tubes as follows: 'original', '10^{-1}', '10^{-2}', '10^{-3}', '10^{-4}' and '10^{-5}'.
2. Use the 10 cm³ graduated pipette and pipette filler to draw up exactly 10 cm³ of the glucose solution. Add the glucose solution to the first test tube, labelled 'original'. This represents '100%' concentration.
3. Using a 1 cm³ pipette and pipette filler, add exactly 1 cm³ of the first dilution into the second test tube. Add distilled water to this second tube to make it up to 10 cm³ and shake well to mix. This concentration is 10^{-1} of the original and the dilution is ×10.
4. Using a clean 1 cm³ pipette and pipette filler, draw up 1 cm³ of the 10^{-1} dilution and add this to the third test tube. Add distilled water to this third tube to make the solution up to 10 cm³ and shake well to mix. This concentration is 10^{-2} of the original and the dilution is $\times 10^2$.
5. Using a clean 1 cm³ pipette and pipette filler, draw up 1 cm³ of the 10^{-2} dilution and add this to the fourth test tube. Make the solution up to 10 cm³ with distilled water and shake well to mix. This concentration is 10^{-3} of the original and the dilution is $\times 10^3$.
6. Using a clean 1 cm³ pipette and pipette filler, draw up 1 cm³ of the 10^{-3} dilution and add this to the fifth test tube. Make the solution up to 10 cm³ with distilled water and shake well to mix. This concentration is 10^{-4} of the original and the dilution is $\times 10^4$.
7. Using a clean 1 cm³ pipette and pipette filler, draw up 1 cm³ of the 10^{-4} dilution and add this to the sixth test tube. Make the solution up to 10 cm³ with distilled water and shake well to mix. This concentration is 10^{-5} of the original and the dilution is $\times 10^5$.

Learning tips

- Do not confuse serial dilutions with a series of dilutions. A series of dilutions is not logarithmic.
- Make sure you use clean pipettes each time you make up a solution, to avoid contamination.

Questions

1 Work out the dilution of the solution in each test tube as a fraction of the original.

2 Making serial dilutions is a precise method for accurately determining the concentration of a solution. Explain why it is important to prevent contamination.

3 Suggest when you might use serial dilutions in an experiment.

PAG 9

CPAC links		Evidence	Done
1a	Correctly follows instructions to carry out the experimental techniques or procedures.	Practical procedure	
2b	Carries out techniques or procedures methodically, in sequence and in combination, identifying practical issues and making adjustments when necessary.	Practical procedure	
3b	Uses appropriate safety equipment and approaches to minimise risks with minimal prompting.	Practical procedure	
4a	Makes accurate observations relevant to the experimental or investigative procedure.	Observations and answers to questions	

Objectives

- To understand and carry out the chemical test for reducing sugars, e.g. glucose
- To estimate the approximate amount of glucose by qualitative analysis

Equipment

- eye protection
- labels, OHP pen or grease pencil
- glucose dilutions: 10%, 1%, 0.1%, 0.01%
- distilled water
- unknown glucose solution
- Benedict's solution
- three 1 cm³ syringes
- six boiling tubes
- boiling tube tongs
- kettle or a pre-set water bath
- 500 cm³ beaker
- 250 cm³ water

Safety 

- Wear eye protection when preparing and using solutions.
- Take care with hot water and hot glassware when using water baths.

Diagram

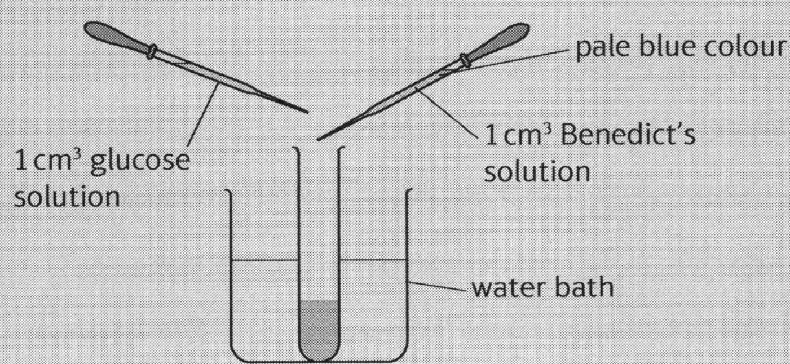

Figure A. Experimental set-up for qualitative testing of a reducing sugar

Learning tips

- Revise how to work out serial dilutions (see Practical 2).
- Find out why glucose is a reducing sugar, i.e. why it changes the colour of Benedict's solution.
- Find out why sucrose is not a reducing sugar.
- Know the reagents and colour changes for reducing sugars, non-reducing sugars, starch, proteins and lipids. (Always state the initial colour and the final colour.) These are often covered in exams.

Procedure

Note: You may be using the glucose solutions that you made in Practical 2. If not, the solutions will be provided for you.

1. Label the five boiling tubes as follows: '10%', '1%', '0.1%', '0.01%' and 'unknown'.
2. Use a syringe to transfer 1 cm³ of the appropriate glucose solution into each boiling tube. Use a clean syringe for each solution.
3. Use a clean syringe to add 1 cm³ of Benedict's solution to the glucose in the first boiling tube. Swirl to mix.
4. Create a hot water bath by filling a beaker with freshly boiled water from a kettle. Place the boiling tube in the water as shown in the diagram. Leave for approximately 5 minutes, or until there is a colour change. Record this colour change in a suitable table.

5 Repeat steps 2–4 for each boiling tube.

6 Repeat steps 2–4 for another boiling tube, using 1 cm^3 of distilled water in place of the glucose. Use a clean syringe. This is the control tube or test.

7 Observe whether there is any colour change in the control tube. Record your observations in the table.

Record your observations here.

Analysis of results

Estimate the approximate glucose percentage of the 'unknown' solution.

....

....

....

....

....

....

Questions

1 What did your results show you about the test for glucose?

....

....

....

....

2 Explain why the test was repeated using distilled water.

....

....

....

....

3 Explain why glucose and Benedict's solution react as they do.

....

....

....

....

....

....

4 Could you measure the concentration of glucose using this method? Explain your answer.

....

....

....

....

....

....

5 How could you modify the method to measure the concentration of reducing sugar?

....

....

....

....

PAG 5 | 9

CPAC links		Evidence	Done
1a	Correctly follows instructions to carry out the experimental techniques or procedures.	Practical procedure	
2b	Carries out techniques or procedures methodically, in sequence and in combination, identifying practical issues and making adjustments when necessary.	Practical procedure	
2d	Selects appropriate equipment and measurement strategies in order to ensure suitably accurate results.	Practical procedure	
4b	Obtains accurate, precise and sufficient data for experimental and investigative procedures and records this methodically using appropriate units and conventions.	Measurements and results table	

Diagram 1

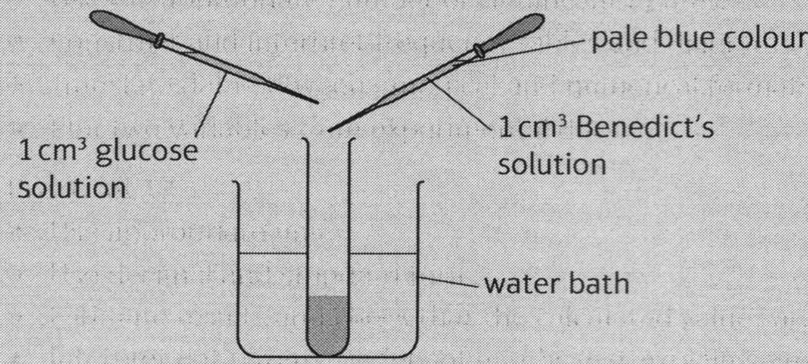

Figure A. Experimental set-up for the preparation of colour standards

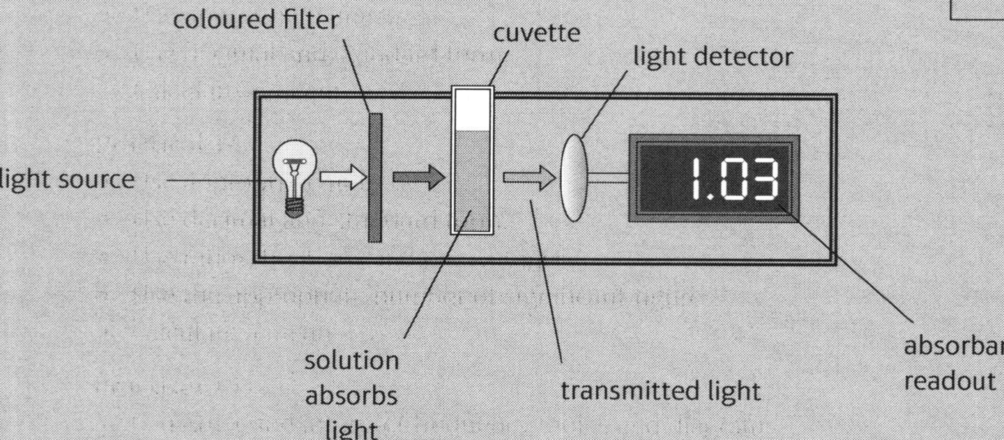

Figure B. Using a colorimeter

Objectives

- To understand and carry out the chemical test for reducing sugars, e.g. glucose
- To estimate the approximate amount of glucose by qualitative analysis

Equipment

- eye protection
- labels, OHP pen or grease pencil
- glucose dilutions: 10%, 1%, 0.1%, 0.01%
- distilled water
- unknown glucose solution (fruit juice)
- Benedict's solution
- three 1 cm^3 syringes
- six boiling tubes
- boiling tube tongs
- kettle or a pre-set water bath
- 500 cm^3 beaker
- 250 cm^3 water

Safety

- Wear eye protection when preparing and using solutions.
- Take care with hot water and hot glassware when using water baths.

Procedure

To prepare the colour standards

1 Label five boiling tubes as follows: 0.1%, 0.5%, 1.0%, 1.5% and 2.0% glucose ($g\,dm^{-3}$).

2 Using a clean syringe, add 5 cm^3 of Benedict's solution to each tube.

3 Add 0.5 cm^3 of each of the glucose solutions to the appropriately labelled boiling tube, using a clean syringe each time.

4 Stir each mixture with a clean, dry glass rod.

5 Create a hot water bath by filling a beaker with freshly boiled water from a kettle. Place all the boiling tubes in the water for 2 minutes, as shown in Figure A. (Alternatively, place the tubes in a pre-set water bath at 80 °C for 9 minutes.)

6 Using tongs, remove the boiling tubes from the water and allow them to cool.

7 Filter the contents of each tube into a clean colorimeter tube or cuvette. You cannot label these tubes, so you must keep them in order so that you know which is which.

8 Take one colorimeter reading for each tube. You will need to use the 4% tube provided to set the colorimeter to zero before each reading.

9 Record the results in the table below.

Glucose concentration (%)	Glucose mass (mg)	Absorbance (arbitrary units)
0.1	0.5	
0.5	2.5	
1	5	
1.5	7.5	
2	10	

To prepare the experimental tube

1 In a clean boiling tube, add 0.5 cm^3 of the fruit juice to 5 cm^3 of Benedict's solution. Heat for 2 minutes in the water bath.

2 Use tongs to remove the tube from the water bath, and allow to cool. Filter the contents into a clean colorimeter tube, then place in the colorimeter and record the absorbance.

....

....

Learning tips

- Be careful not to leave fingerprints on the colorimeter tubes as this could affect the transmission of light.
- Colour filters are used for greater accuracy.

Analysis of results

- Plot a graph of absorbance against mass of glucose. This provides a calibration curve.
- Use the graph to read the mass of glucose present in the fruit juice.

....

Plot your graph here.

Questions

1 What is the glucose content of the fruit juice in milligrams?

2 Why is the reducing sugar content of the fruit juice likely to be different from the glucose content?

3 Why is it important to test each concentration in exactly the same way?

4 What did you notice about the residue left in the filter for each solution tested? How could you use this as the basis for another way of measuring the concentration of glucose in an unknown solution?

5 Explain any difficulties you had in carrying out the task. State what improvements you would make if you performed the experiment again.

PAG 4

CPAC links		Evidence	Done
1a	Correctly follows instructions to carry out the experimental techniques or procedures.	Practical procedure	
2b	Carries out techniques or procedures methodically, in sequence and in combination, identifying practical issues and making adjustments when necessary.	Practical procedure	
2d	Selects appropriate equipment and measurement strategies in order to ensure suitably accurate results.	Practical procedure	
3b	Uses appropriate safety equipment and approaches to minimise risks with minimal prompting.	Practical procedure	
4b	Obtains accurate, precise and sufficient data for experimental and investigative procedures and records this methodically using appropriate units and conventions.	Measurements and results table	

Objectives

- To investigate the catalase activity of celery
- To determine the effect of substrate concentration on catalase activity

Equipment

- eye protection and disposable gloves
- celery extract
- hydrogen peroxide stock solution, at 20 vol
- distilled water
- six test tubes
- two 5 cm^3 syringes
- 1 cm^3 syringe
- six glass rods
- watch glass
- forceps
- stop clock
- paper discs cut from filter paper
- small beaker and paper towel to rinse
- labels, OHP pen or grease pencil

Safety 

- Eye protection must be worn as hydrogen peroxide is harmful.
- Disposable gloves should be worn as hydrogen peroxide can damage the skin.
- Hydrogen peroxide (H_2O_2) is an irritant.
- Concentrated catalase is an irritant.
- Take care when handling glassware.

Irritant

Harmful

Corrosive

Procedure

1 Using one 5 cm^3 syringe for distilled water and the other for hydrogen peroxide, make up dilutions of hydrogen peroxide in the test tubes. Use the table to help you make your dilutions.

Concentration 20 vol H_2O_2 (%)	Volume of water (cm^3)	Volume of H_2O_2 (cm^3)
100	0	10
80	2	8
60	4	6
40	6	4
20	8	2
0	10	0

2 Each test tube should now contain 10 cm^3 of a hydrogen peroxide dilution. Label the tubes appropriately.

3 Using the 1 cm^3 syringe, transfer 1 cm^3 of celery extract into a watch glass. Soak three discs of filter paper in the extract for 5 minutes.

4 Prepare a suitable results table in the space provided to record times for each of the hydrogen peroxide dilutions.

5 Use the forceps to remove one of the paper discs and gently shake it to remove any enzyme drips.

6 Drop the paper disc into the first hydrogen peroxide dilution. Use a clean glass rod to push the disc to the bottom, if necessary.

7 As soon as the disc hits the bottom of the tube, start the stop clock. Time how long it takes for the disc to rise to the surface of the hydrogen peroxide.

8 Remove the disc and repeat with the other two discs, each time in the same hydrogen peroxide solution.

9 Discard the celery extract and transfer another 1 cm^3 of fresh celery extract into the watch glass.

10 Soak three more discs in the fresh celery extract for 5 minutes. Repeat steps 5–8 for the second dilution of hydrogen peroxide.

11 Repeat the procedure with three discs for each hydrogen peroxide dilution.

12 Record the results in a table and calculate the mean time for the discs to rise in each dilution.

Learning tips

- The gas bubbles that form on the discs are the product of the breakdown reaction between catalase in the celery and the hydrogen peroxide.
- Find out what this gas is and write out the chemical reaction.
- Repeated readings allow the mean to be calculated and increase the reliability of the data.

Analysis of results

Calculate a mean for each concentration and plot a suitable graph of the mean.

Record your results and calculations here.

Plot your graph here.

Questions

1 Discuss your findings and the shape of the graph.

....

....

....

2 What caused the paper discs to rise to the surface of the hydrogen peroxide?

....

....

....

3 Explain the results obtained for the different substrate concentrations using your biological knowledge.

....

....

....

....

....

....

....

....

4 The limitations of an investigation are factors that reduce the accuracy and reliability of results. They may arise from variables that are difficult to control. What are the limitations of this procedure?

....

....

....

....

....

....

....

....

5 How could you improve the investigation and overcome some of the limitations?

....

....

....

....

....

....

PAG 4

CPAC links		Evidence	Done
2a	Correctly uses appropriate instrumentation, apparatus and materials (including ICT) to carry out investigative activities, experimental techniques and procedures with minimal assistance or prompting.	Practical procedure	
2d	Selects appropriate equipment and measurement strategies in order to ensure suitably accurate results.	Answers to questions	
3b	Uses appropriate safety equipment and approaches to minimise risks with minimal prompting.	Practical procedure	
4b	Obtains accurate, precise and sufficient data for experimental and investigative procedures and records this methodically using appropriate units and conventions.	Measurements and results table	

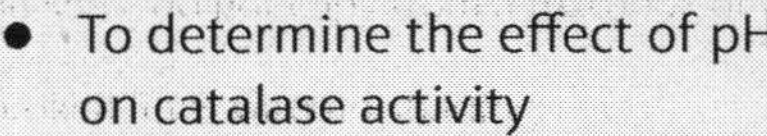

Objective

- To determine the effect of pH on catalase activity

Equipment

- eye protection and disposable gloves
- catalase solution
- 150 cm^3 10 vol hydrogen peroxide
- distilled water
- five test tubes with side-arms, rubber bungs, connecting tubes and delivery tubes
- five 100 cm^3 measuring cylinders/burettes
- five large beakers to act as water troughs
- two 10 cm^3 syringes
- five 1 cm^3 syringes
- five stop clocks
- five pH buffers: pH 4, pH 5, pH 6, pH 7 and pH 8
- labels, OHP pen or grease pencil

Safety 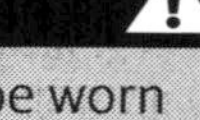

- Eye protection must be worn as hydrogen peroxide is harmful.
- Disposable gloves should be worn as hydrogen peroxide can damage the skin.
- Hydrogen peroxide (H_2O_2) is an irritant.
- Concentrated catalase is an irritant.
- Take care when handling glassware.

Diagram

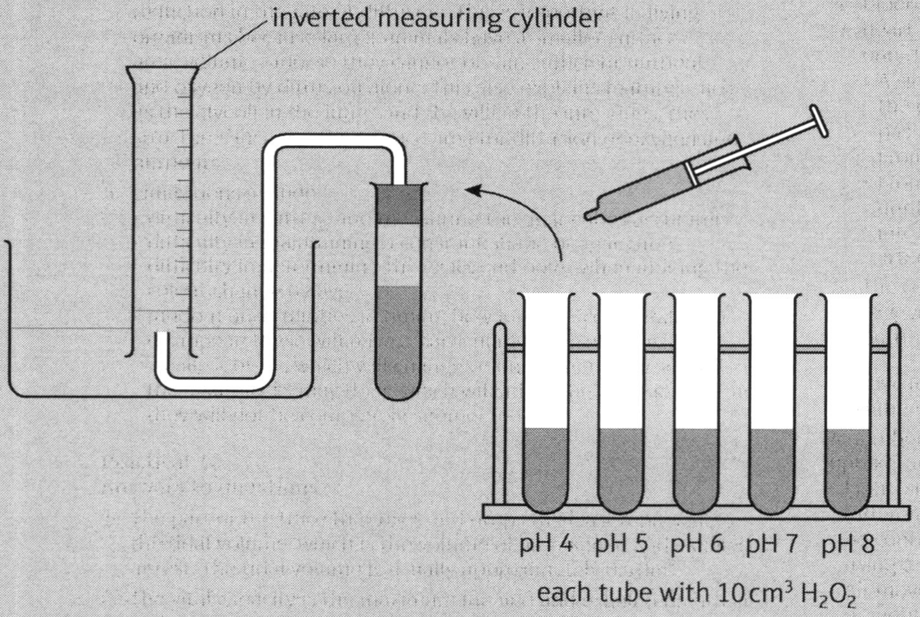

Figure A. Experimental set-up to investigate the effect of pH on catalase activity

Procedure

1 Fill five 100 cm^3 measuring cylinders with water and invert each one in a separate large beaker.

2 Insert a delivery tube into the open end of each measuring cylinder under the water, as shown in Figure A.

3 Label five test tubes with the pH buffers 4, 5, 6, 7 and 8. Add 1 cm^3 of the appropriate pH buffer to each test tube, using a clean 1 cm^3 syringe each time.

4 Using a clean 10 cm^3 syringe, add 10 cm^3 of hydrogen peroxide to each test tube.

5 Using a clean 10 cm^3 syringe, quickly add 1 cm^3 of the enzyme (catalase) to the first test tube and insert the rubber bung and the side-arm delivery tube. Start the first stop clock. It is important to do this step as quickly as possible.

6 Make sure the other end of the delivery tube is completely under the inverted measuring cylinder.

7 Repeat steps 5 and 6 for each test tube in turn, using a new stop clock for each test tube.

8 After 15 minutes on each stop clock, stop the clock and read off the volume of gas collected in the corresponding test tube.

9 Record your results in a suitable table.

Learning tips

- pH is a measure of the concentration of hydrogen ions present in a solution.
- Enzymes are affected by changes in pH because the hydrogen ions disrupt the hydrogen bonds and the ionic bonds that hold the tertiary structure of the active site in place. This causes the active site to change shape, so the substrate molecules no longer fit.

Record your results here.

Analysis of results

- Plot a suitable graph of reaction rate against pH and determine the optimum pH for catalase.
- Describe your graph. What is the effect of pH on the rate of catalase activity?

....

....

....

Plot your graph here.

Questions

1 Which gas is produced in this reaction? Write a balanced equation for the reaction.

2 Explain why changes in pH alter the rate of an enzyme-controlled reaction.

3 Using your biological knowledge, explain why different enzymes are affected by pH changes in different ways.

4 Identify any anomalous results and explain why you have these anomalies.

5 What are the main limitations of this procedure and how will they affect the data?

6 How could you reduce the limitations and improve the accuracy of the data?

PAG 4

CPAC links		Evidence	Done
1a	Correctly follows instructions to carry out the experimental techniques or procedures.	Practical procedure	
2b	Carries out techniques or procedures methodically, in sequence and in combination, identifying practical issues and making adjustments when necessary.	Practical procedure	
2c	Identifies and controls significant quantitative variables where applicable, and plans approaches to take account of variables that cannot readily be controlled.	Practical procedure and answers to questions	
4a	Makes accurate observations relevant to the experimental or investigative procedure.	Observations and results table	
4b	Obtains accurate, precise and sufficient data for experimental and investigative procedures and records this methodically using appropriate units and conventions.	Measurements and results table	

Objectives

- To investigate the effect of temperature on amylase activity
- To investigate the hydrolysis of starch with amylase

Equipment

- eye protection
- water baths at 0 °C, 20 °C, 40 °C, 60 °C and 80 °C
- 10 cm^3 syringe
- 50 cm^3 buffered starch solution at 0.5% concentration
- five boiling tubes
- 1 cm^3 syringe
- 20 cm^3 amylase at 1% concentration
- five test tubes, test tube rack
- labels, OHP pen or grease pencil
- five dropping pipettes
- five spotting tiles
- iodine solution (with pipette)
- glass rod
- stop clock
- beaker of rinsing water and paper towel

Safety

- Wear eye protection.
- The solutions used may be irritants and allergens.
- Take care to avoid scalds from hot water.

Diagram

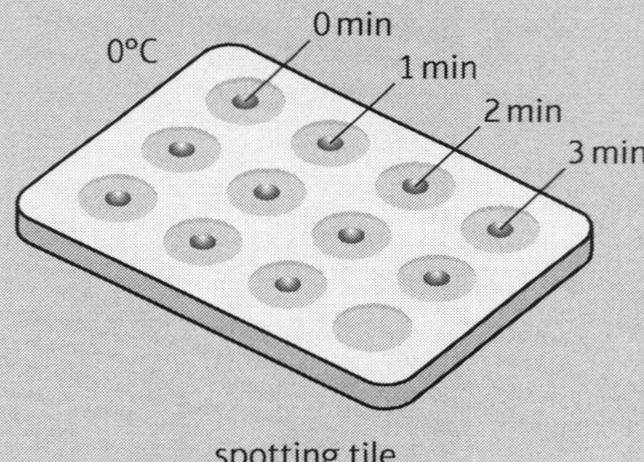

Figure A. Use of a spotting tile to investigate the effect of temperature on amylase activity

Learning tip

Clean your glass rod before each use to avoid contamination.

Procedure

1 Prepare the water baths as instructed by your teacher.

2 Label the five boiling tubes 0 °C, 20 °C, 40 °C, 60 °C and 80 °C. Use the large syringe to add 10 cm^3 of starch to each boiling tube and place each tube in the corresponding pre-set water bath.

3 Label the five test tubes 0 °C, 20 °C, 40 °C, 60 °C and 80 °C. Use the small syringe to add 1 cm^3 of amylase to each test tube and place each tube in the corresponding water bath.

4 Leave all the tubes for 5 minutes. Meanwhile, prepare a table for your results in the space provided and add two drops of iodine solution to each well of your spotting tiles.

5 After 5 minutes, pour the test tube of enzyme at 0 °C into the boiling tube of starch at 0 °C. Stir with a glass rod and start the stop clock.

6 Immediately remove a small sample of the mixture with a pipette and add two drops to the first well of your first spotting tile.

7 Continue taking samples from the mixture every minute up to a maximum of 10 minutes, adding two drops to the next well of the spotting tile each time.

8 Repeat steps 5–7 for the tubes at each temperature, using a different spotting tile each time. You will need to stagger your tests, so leave 5 minutes before you mix the enzyme and starch for the next temperature. Be careful not to confuse the different tests, as they will overlap.

9 Record all your results in the table you have prepared.

Analysis of results

- Calculate the reaction rate for each temperature.
- Plot a graph of reaction rate against temperature.
- Describe your graph. What is the effect of temperature on the rate of catalase activity?

....

....

....

Record your results and calculations here.

Plot your graph here.

Questions

1 Explain why the starch was made up with a buffer solution.

2 Why were all the boiling tubes and test tubes left in the water baths for 5 minutes before the enzyme was mixed with the starch?

3 State three variables that were controlled in this investigation.

4 Use your biological knowledge to describe and explain the results you have obtained for the different temperatures.

5 What are the main limitations of this technique? Where possible, suggest an improvement for each limitation given.

PAG 5 | 8

CPAC links		Evidence	Done
2a	Correctly uses appropriate instrumentation, apparatus and materials (including ICT) to carry out investigative activities, experimental techniques and procedures with minimal assistance or prompting.	Practical procedure	
2c	Identifies and controls significant quantitative variables where applicable, and plans approaches to take account of variables that cannot readily be controlled.	Practical procedure and answers to questions	
3b	Uses appropriate safety equipment and approaches to minimise risks with minimal prompting.	Practical procedure	
4b	Obtains accurate, precise and sufficient data for experimental and investigative procedures and records this methodically using appropriate units and conventions.	Practical procedure and results table	
5a	Uses appropriate software and/ or tools to process data, carry out research and report findings.	Processed data	

Objectives

- To investigate the effect of temperature on cellular membranes
- To determine from this some properties of membranes

Equipment

- eye protection, lab coat, disposable gloves
- water baths, pre-set to the required temperatures
- thermometer
- distilled water buffered to pH 7
- large beetroot (one per student)
- cork borer size no. 5
- ruler
- white tile
- knife
- syringe
- pipettes
- test tubes
- colorimeter
- cuvettes
- labels
- waterproof marker pen
- forceps
- stop clock
- paper towels

Safety

- Take care with sharp items such as cork borers and knives.
- Take care with hot water in baths above 40 °C.
- Avoid direct contact between water and the electrical components of, for example, water baths and colorimeters.

Diagram

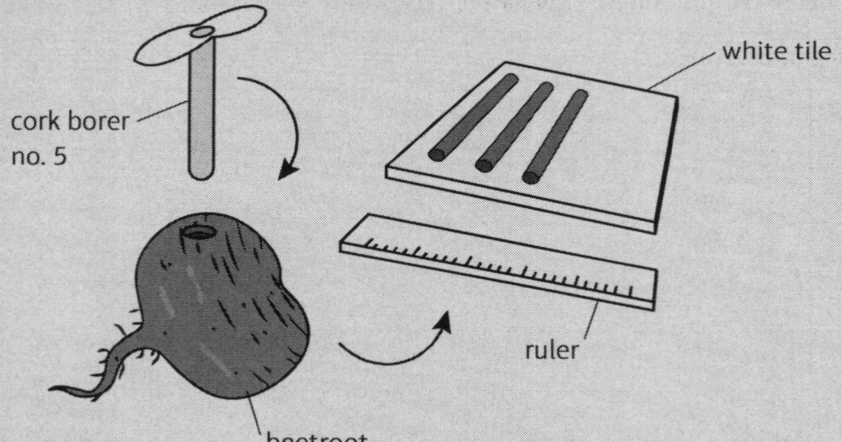

Figure A. Equipment for investigating the effect of temperature on membrane permeability

Procedure

1. Prepare six water baths pre-set to a range of temperatures between 30 and 80 °C.
2. Label six test tubes with the temperatures of the six water baths. Use a syringe to add 10 cm^3 of distilled water (buffered to pH 7) to each test tube.
3. Place each tube into the water bath with the corresponding temperature for 5 minutes.
4. Check the temperature is correct using a thermometer.

5 Cut six beetroot cylinders using a cork borer size no. 5. Using a knife, ruler and white tile, trim the cylinders to the same length (e.g. 40 mm). Wash the cylinders thoroughly with distilled water for 5 minutes and pat dry with a paper towel.

6 Add one beetroot cylinder to each test tube and leave for 15 minutes.

7 Shake the tubes once and then, using forceps, carefully remove the beetroot cylinder from each tube and discard.

8 Decant enough liquid from each test tube to fill a colorimeter cuvette exactly. Fill one cuvette from each test tube – six cuvettes in total.

9 Set the colorimeter to green filter and absorption. Zero the colorimeter using a blank cuvette filled with distilled water.

10 Place each cuvette in turn into the colorimeter and read the absorption, recording your results in a suitable table.

Learning tip

Think of beetroot cells as membrane sacks that hold in the pink pigment under 'normal' conditions and revise what you have learned about membrane structure, e.g. are they weak and fluid or solid and strong?

Record your results and calculations here.

Analysis of results

- Plot a graph of your results to show the relationship between temperature and absorbance.
- If repeats or pooled class data are available, plot the mean values for each temperature on the same graph.
- Include standard deviation error bars if your teacher instructs you to.

Plot your graph here.

Questions

1 How variable were the class results? Suggest reasons for any variation.

2 Suggest why the tubes are placed in the water baths for 5 minutes before the cylinders of beetroot are added.

3 Why are the cylinders washed with distilled water and dried before the experiment is started?

4 Which variables are controlled during the experiment?

5 Use the trend line of your graph to describe the effect of temperature on the per cent transmission between 30 °C and 80 °C.

....

....

....

....

....

....

6 Explain your results in terms of membrane structure. What is happening to the beetroot membrane during this experiment?

....

....

....

....

....

....

7 From the graph, explain why the absorption changes significantly at one particular temperature.

....

....

....

....

....

....

....

....

....

....

....

....

....

....

....

PAG 8

CPAC links		Evidence	Done
2a	Correctly uses appropriate instrumentation, apparatus and materials (including ICT) to carry out investigative activities, experimental techniques and procedures with minimal assistance or prompting.	Practical procedure	
4a	Makes accurate observations relevant to the experimental or investigative procedure.	Drawings and results table	

Objectives

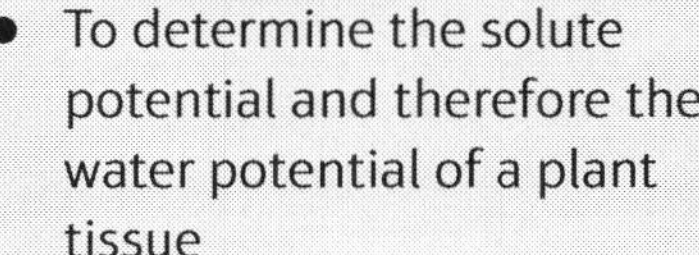

- To determine the solute potential and therefore the water potential of a plant tissue
- To determine the effect of water potential on onion tissue

Equipment

- plant tissue such as an onion epidermis, or leaves with a single cell layer, e.g. from pond weed or moss
- five glucose solutions (with concentrations ranging from 0.1 mol dm^{-3} to 0.9 mol dm^{-3}) or five salt solutions (ranging from 0.1% to 2%, with one at 0.9%)
- distilled water
- five watch glasses
- dropping pipettes
- filter paper
- forceps/scalpel
- labels, OHP pen (permanent) or grease pencil
- microscope, slides, coverslips

Safety

- Take care with glassware and sharps.

Diagram

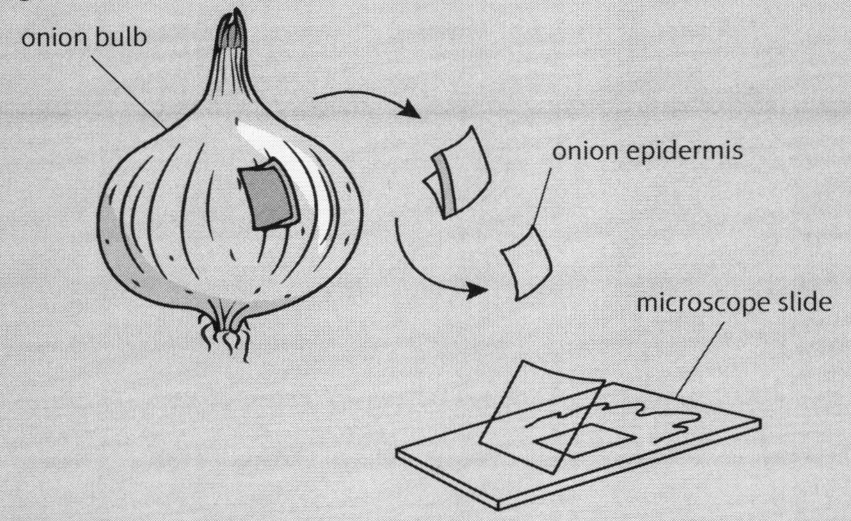

Figure A. Equipment for finding the water potential of onion tissue

Procedure

1. Take five thin sections of the plant tissue (1 cm^2 is a suitable size to use). The tissue must be only one cell thick, so that the cells can be examined clearly.
2. Using a grease pencil or an OHP pen, label five watch glasses and five microscope slides with the different concentrations of salt or glucose solution.
3. Pipette some of each salt or glucose solution into the appropriate watch glass.
4. Place one of the five tissue sections into each of the watch glasses and leave for 20 minutes.
5. Remove each tissue section from the watch glass with forceps. Place each tissue section onto the slide labelled with the appropriate concentration of salt or glucose solution. Put a drop of the corresponding solution onto the slide and float the tissue onto it.
6. Carefully cover each tissue section with a coverslip and observe under the microscope.
7. Count 25 cells in each tissue section and decide how many of these cells show plasmolysis. Record your findings in a suitable table in the space provided.

8 The solution in which close to 50% of cells show plasmolysis shows the closest value to the solute potential of the cells.

9 If you have time, this is a good opportunity to practise drawing cells. Draw plasmolysed cells, showing how the plasma membrane separates from the cell wall. You can use the space provided to do this.

10 Irrigate a slide that is showing plasmolysis, using distilled water. This is best done by adding distilled water to the edge of the coverslip using a dropping pipette, while drawing the solution with a piece of filter paper at the opposite edge of the coverslip.

11 Observe the changes that have occurred after 5 minutes and record your observations in the table you have prepared.

Tips for good biological drawings

- Use a sharp HB pencil. Keep lines clear and continuous, not feathery or sketched.
- Draw only what you see. Do not draw stylised patterns, and do not make it up!
- Start with an outline. Keep it large and think about proportions.
- Do not use shading or colour.
- Draw label lines in pencil with a ruler. Lines should not have arrowheads and should just touch the item to be labelled.

Use this space to draw your diagrams.

Record your results and calculations here.

Learning tips

- Scientists presuppose that the solution that causes 50% of the cells to plasmolyse is equivalent to the solution that would cause all the cells to just begin plasmolysis.
- Be familiar with the formula:

  water potential = solute potential + pressure potential
- When 50% of the cells are plasmolysed, the water potential and solute potential are the same. At this point, there is no pressure on the cell walls so the pressure potential is zero.

Analysis of results

- Calculate the percentage of cells showing plasmolysis for each concentration. If possible, collect results from other students as replicates at each concentration and then calculate a mean.

....

....

....

....

....

....

- Draw a graph showing the percentage of plasmolysed cells against the concentration of the solution.

Plot your graph here.

- From your graph, determine the solute concentration that would cause exactly 50% plasmolysis.

- Osmotic potential is measured in kPa. Use the table below to estimate the solute potential of the onion tissue and, from this, the water potential of the tissue.

Table 1 Relationship between molarity and osmotic potential of salt solutions

Concentration of sucrose solution (mol dm^{-3})	Solute potential (kPa)
0.05	−130
0.10	−260
0.15	−410
0.20	−540
0.25	−680
0.30	−820
0.35	−970
0.40	−1120
0.45	−1280
0.50	−1450
0.55	−1620
0.60	−1800
0.65	−1980
0.70	−2180
0.75	−2370
0.80	−2580

Questions

1 **a** Which solution is closest to 50% plasmolysis?

b What can you conclude about the concentration of the external solution and the concentration of the cell contents at this point?

2 Why are water potential and solute potential only the same when 50% of the cells are plasmolysed?

3 What is the estimated water potential of your onion tissue?

4 What observations did you make after irrigating the slide and showing plasmolysis with water?

5 Write a short evaluation of the investigative methods. Were there any areas of inaccuracy or possible errors?

PAG 1

CPAC links		Evidence	Done
2d	Selects appropriate equipment and measurement strategies in order to ensure suitably accurate results.	Use of graticule	
3a	Identifies hazards and assesses risks associated with these hazards, making safety adjustments as necessary, when carrying out experimental techniques and procedures in the lab or field.	Risk assessment	
4a	Makes accurate observations relevant to the experimental or investigative procedure.	Drawings	
4b	Obtains accurate, precise and sufficient data for experimental and investigative procedures and records this methodically using appropriate units and conventions.	Measurements and results table	

Objective 

- To observe the stages of the cell cycle in living tissue

Equipment

- eye protection, lab coat, disposable gloves
- growing root tips from, for example, an onion bulb or a bean seedling
- glass slides and coverslips
- scalpel
- ruler
- hot plate
- watch glass and marker pen
- acetic orcein
- a mixture of acetic orcein and HCl
- dissecting needle
- filter paper
- lamp
- microscope
- pre-prepared slides

Safety 

- Eye protection must be worn.
- Take care with glassware and sharps.
- Take particular care when tapping or pressing on slides/coverslips.
- HCl is an irritant at 2 mol dm^{-3}.
- Acetic orcein is corrosive.

Irritant

Corrosive

Diagram

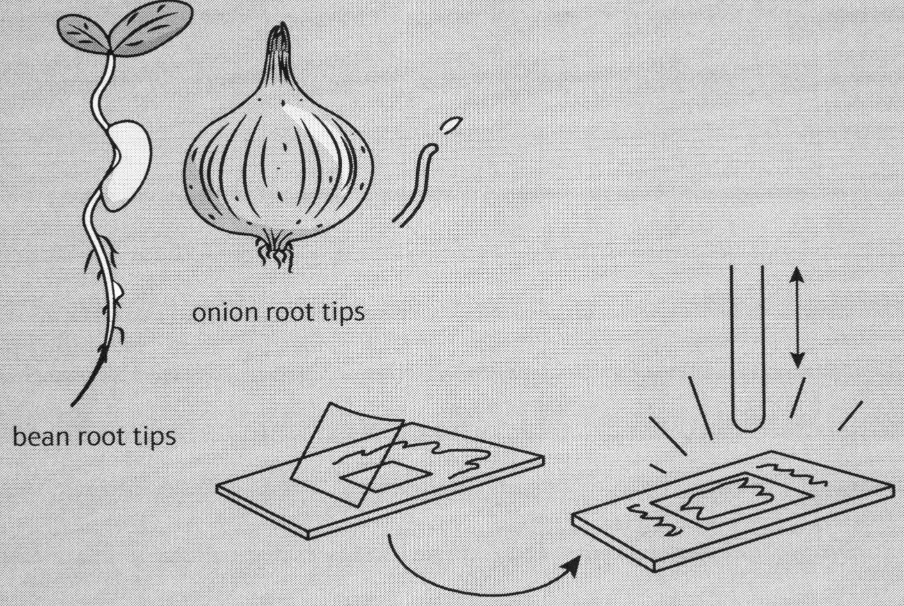

Figure A. Equipment used to observe mitosis

Learning tips

- To see mitosis in action, you need to look at living cells. Most plants (e.g. garlic, onions, beans) grow roots that have actively dividing cells in their tips. Each cell has only a few chromosomes (e.g. eight in garlic bulbs) so it is relatively easy to see the chromosomes once they have condensed.
- In order to see the chromosomes inside the cells, you must separate the cells and spread them out into a layer that is ideally just one cell thick.
- Remember that your preparation stops the process of mitosis at one point in time. You will not see mitosis taking place; rather, you will see a snapshot of many cells, each stopped at whatever stage it happened to be in. Most of the chromosomes you can see will be heavily stained – they will not look like the usual view depicted in diagrams of living cells with organelles.

Risk assessment

- You should complete your own risk assessment prior to this practical.
- Read the outline of the practical and make sure you understand the information about the reagents used.
- Assess risk by identifying hazards and considering the likelihood of problems. Suggest suitable control measures to reduce risk.
- Ask your teacher to check your risk assessment before you begin the practical.

Write your risk assessment here, then get it checked.

Procedure

1 Take a whole root and cut 15 mm off three growing root tips.

2 Place the cut tips in a watch glass and cover with a mixture of acetic orcein stain and HCl. Carefully note and follow which end is the growing tip (mark the watch glass if necessary).

3 Place the watch glass on a hot plate for 5 minutes to warm the cells at the tips.

4 Carefully remove the tips from the watch glass and place them on a clean glass slide.

5 Taking care not to break the slide, cut off 3 mm from the tip of each root (not the cut end!) and discard the rest.

6 Place one 3 mm tip on a new glass slide and add three drops of acetic orcein stain to cover it. Then cover with the coverslip.

7 Use the handle of the dissecting needle to tap the tip gently (through the coverslip) to break up the tissues.

8 Wrap several layers of filter paper tightly around the slide and the coverslip.

9 Press gently on the paper to squash the tissues. Take care not to twist the slide as you press down.

10 Repeat steps 6–9 for the other two 3 mm tips.

11 Examine each slide under the microscope on low power to identify the area of dividing cells. Then turn up to a higher power.

12 Examine each preparation carefully for cells undergoing different stages of mitosis. Identify the different stages by comparing what you can see with a photograph of cells during mitosis. Identify cells in the following stages of the cell cycle: interphase, prophase, metaphase, anaphase and telophase. Bear in mind that mitosis is a dynamic process, so some cells may have been fixed in transition from one stage to the next. You will have to interpret what you see.

13 For each slide, count the number of cells in the area visible under the microscope when viewed at ×400 (the field of view). Count the number of cells in each stage of mitosis. Record your results in a table.

14 If time allows, make labelled drawings of one cell from each of the stages you have identified. Your drawings will be simple outlines of the cells and the groups of chromosomes in them – few other structures will be visible. Aim to show the relative sizes and positions of the chromosomes and the cell accurately. Annotate your drawings to describe what is happening. These drawings may be made later from prepared slides.

15 Calibrate your eyepiece graticule with a stage graticule as shown in Figure B.

16 Use the graticule in the microscope to measure the width of the cells you are drawing and the length of the chromosomes. These measurements may be made later from prepared slides.

17 Add a scale bar to each drawing.

Using the microscope graticule

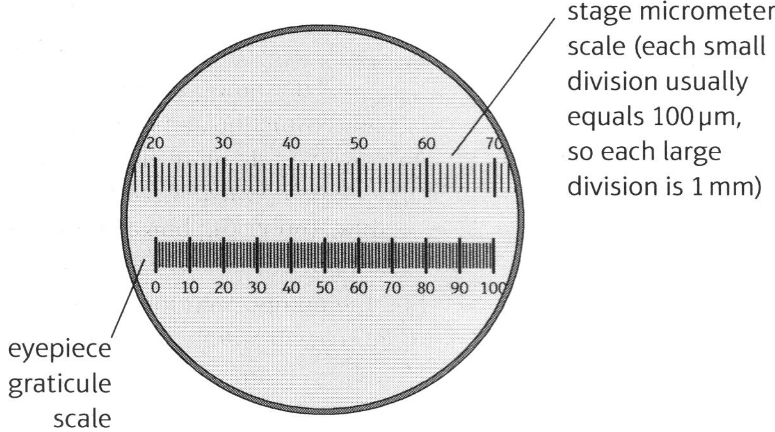

Figure B. Calibrating the stage micrometer using an eyepiece graticule

- Using the low-power objective, focus on the micrometer scale. The smallest division of the micrometer scale is usually 100 µm.
- Move the slide and rotate the eyepiece to align the scales of the eyepiece graticule and the stage micrometer in the field of view.
- Count the number of divisions (eyepiece units or epu) on the eyepiece graticule that are equivalent to a known length on the micrometer slide. This will allow you to work out the length of each eyepiece unit. For example, if 100 µm is equivalent to 4 epu, then each epu is 100/4 = 25 µm at this magnification.
- Repeat this for the medium- and high-power objectives.

Record your results and measurements here.

Tips for good biological drawings

- Use a sharp HB pencil. Keep lines clear and continuous, not feathery or sketched.
- Draw only what you see. Do not draw stylised patterns, and do not make it up!
- Start with an outline. Keep it large and think about proportions.
- Do not use shading or colour.
- Draw label lines in pencil with a ruler. Lines should not have arrowheads and should just touch the item to be labelled.

Use this space to draw your diagrams (leave space to record your measurements).

Analysis of results

- Calculate the percentage of the cells in each stage of mitosis. Add the percentages to your table.

- Rank these values from highest to lowest.

- Arrange your diagrams in the correct sequence for mitosis.
- Calculate magnifications for your drawings and the width (in micrometres) of a cell.

Questions

1 What do the percentages suggest to you about the length of time a cell spends in each stage of mitosis? Explain how you arrived at your conclusion.

2 Explain why the root tip is heated with acid.

3 Why is it important not to twist the microscope slide as you press down?

4 What effect will pressing the slide preparation have on the dividing cells?

5 Suggest improvements to this method that would allow you to accurately compare the size of cells in different stages of mitosis.

PAG 8

CPAC links		Evidence	Done
2a	Correctly uses appropriate instrumentation, apparatus and materials (including ICT) to carry out investigative activities, experimental techniques and procedures with minimal assistance or prompting.	Practical procedure	
2b	Carries out techniques or procedures methodically, in sequence and in combination, identifying practical issues and making adjustments when necessary.	Practical procedure	
2c	Identifies and controls significant quantitative variables where applicable, and plans approaches to take account of variables that cannot readily be controlled.	Planning and practical procedure	
3b	Uses appropriate safety equipment and approaches to minimise risks with minimal prompting.	Practical procedure	
4b	Obtains accurate, precise and sufficient data for experimental and investigative procedures and records this methodically using appropriate units and conventions.	Measurements and results table	

Objectives

- To calculate the surface area : volume ratio (*SA* : *V*)
- To show the effect of the surface area : volume ratio on the diffusion rate of hydrochloric acid

Equipment

- eye protection, disposable gloves
- a block of stained agar of depth 10 mm
- single-edged razor blade or scalpel
- five test tubes, test tube rack/ small beakers
- labels or grease pencil/OHP pen
- forceps
- 2 mol dm^{-3} hydrochloric acid (HCl)
- 5 cm^3 syringe
- white tile
- ruler or callipers
- stop clock

Safety

- 2 mol dm^{-3} hydrochloric acid is an irritant and corrosive so eye protection must be worn.
- Sharps may cut the skin if mishandled so care must be taken.
- Use and dispose of gloves correctly.

Irritant

Harmful

Corrosive

Procedure

Read the procedure below. Identify at least three key factors that may affect the diffusion rate and should be controlled in this experiment.

....

....

....

....

....

....

....

1. Use a sharp razor, a clear ruler or callipers, and a white tile to cut the agar into five cubes with different side lengths (from 2 mm to 10 mm).
2. Carefully use the razor blade to lift the agar blocks. Use the forceps to place each block into a test tube or beaker. Label each test tube or beaker clearly with the size of agar block.
3. Using a syringe, cover each block with 2 cm^3 of 2 mol dm^{-3} HCl, so that it is immersed.
4. Start the stop clock and time how long it takes for the pink colour to disappear from each block, so that the block is completely colourless.
5. Record the results in a suitable table.

Learning tip

The surface area: volume ratio affects diffusion rates in living organisms.

Record your results here.

Analysis of results

- Draw a suitable graph to show the effect of the surface area: volume ratio on the rate of diffusion.
- Describe the relationship shown by your graph.

....

....

....

....

Plot your graph here.

Questions

1 What could you predict about the effect of the surface area:volume ratio on the rate of diffusion?

....

....

2 Describe the relationship between the shortest distance to the centre of the cube and the time taken for the HCl to diffuse to the centre. Is there any approximate numerical relationship? For example, what happens to the diffusion time if the distance doubles?

....

....

....

....

....

3 What additional procedures could you carry out to make your results more reliable?

....

....

4 Explain the effect of the surface area:volume ratio on the rate of diffusion. How is this important in living organisms? Use your graph and your scientific knowledge to support your answer.

....

....

....

....

....

5 What are the limitations of this experiment?

....

....

....

....

....

....

....

....

....

PAG 10

CPAC links		Evidence	Done
1a	Correctly follows instructions to carry out the experimental techniques or procedures.	Practical procedure	
2a	Correctly uses appropriate instrumentation, apparatus and materials (including ICT) to carry out investigative activities, experimental techniques and procedures with minimal assistance or prompting.	Practical procedure	
4b	Obtains accurate, precise and sufficient data for experimental and investigative procedures and records this methodically using appropriate units and conventions.	Practical procedure and results table	

Objectives

- To measure tidal volume and vital capacity of the lungs using a spirometer
- To record and read data from a spirometer

Equipment

- eye protection, disposable gloves
- spirometer
- sterile mouthpiece and nose clip
- oxygen cylinder (medical grade)
- connecting tube
- motion sensor, datalogger and computer
- soda lime or *Carbosorb*

Safety

- Await instructions from your teacher before attempting to use the spirometer.
- A sterile mouthpiece must be used for each student.
- This practical may not be suitable for students with asthma.
- Soda lime is corrosive.

Diagram

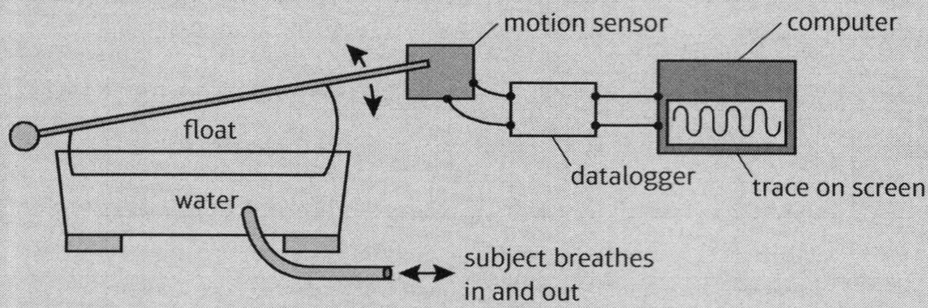

Figure A. A spirometer and datalogger

Procedure

1 The spirometer should already have been set up and checked by a technician. The air chamber should be filled with medical grade oxygen.

2 Before you start, check that the sensor and the datalogger are correctly positioned to record any changes in the air chamber as you breathe.

3 Calibrate the volume by filling the air chamber with a litre of oxygen. Your teacher will tell you how to do this.

4 Sit quietly for 5 minutes before starting the breathing experiments.

5 Carefully place the clip on your nose to prevent air entering or leaving through your nose. Breathe in and out through your mouth, with the nose clip in place, while the spirometer is connected to the atmosphere. When you are comfortable, switch the machine to the oxygen supply.

6 Take a sterile mouthpiece and continue to breathe normally through your mouth, into and out of the mouthpiece, which is attached to the spirometer.

7 Continue breathing into and out of the mouthpiece for 1 minute or until your teacher asks you to stop.

8 When you are comfortable, take the deepest possible breath in. When you breathe out again, force as much air as possible into the mouthpiece. Do this only once and then return to normal breathing.

8 Examine the spirometer trace.

Learning tip

Make sure you understand the terms 'tidal volume' and 'vital capacity'.

Analysis of results

- Using the traces from a datalogger output, you can measure and count the depth and number of breaths. Several parameters can be analysed, such as rate of breathing, changes in rate, depth of breathing, tidal volume and vital capacity.

Record your results and processed data here.

Questions

1 According to the spirometer trace, how much air does a person take in with each breath during normal breathing?

2 What is vital capacity and which part of the trace shows this measurement?

3 What is your vital capacity reading from the trace?

4 Why is it not possible to measure total lung capacity from the trace?

5 Why do the peaks and troughs get lower on the trace?

6 Calculate the total amount of air taken in with each breath.

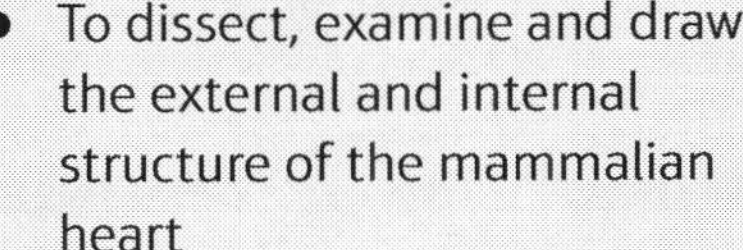

CPAC links		Evidence	Done
1a	Correctly follows instructions to carry out the experimental techniques or procedures.	Practical procedure	
2a	Correctly uses appropriate instrumentation, apparatus and materials (including ICT) to carry out investigative activities, experimental techniques and procedures with minimal assistance or prompting.	Practical procedure	
3b	Uses appropriate safety equipment and approaches to minimise risks with minimal prompting.	Practical procedure	
4a	Makes accurate observations relevant to the experimental or investigative procedure.	Observations, drawing and measurements	

Objective

- To dissect, examine and draw the external and internal structure of the mammalian heart

Equipment

- disposable protective apron and disposable plastic/rubber gloves
- fresh sheep or pig heart
- wax dissection tray
- scissors
- mounted needle
- ruler or callipers with millimetre divisions
- paper towel
- blunt seeker
- disinfectant solution and plastic bags

Safety

- Wear a disposable apron to protect your clothing.
- Take care when using sharps to avoid cutting your hands.
- Wear gloves when handling hearts and wash your hands thoroughly after the practical. Dispose of used gloves immediately.

Diagram

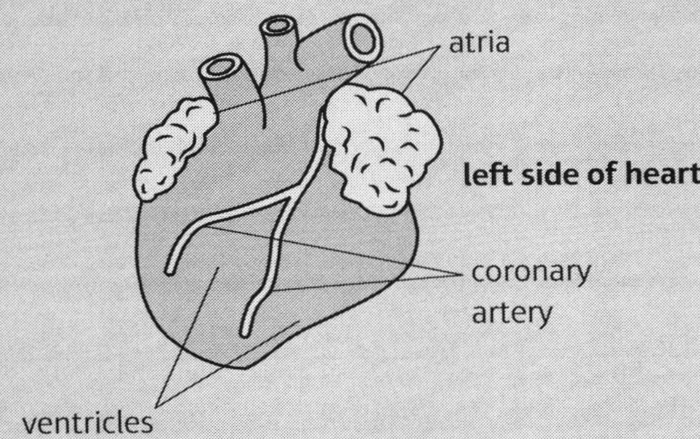

Figure A. A diagram of a mammalian heart

Procedure

1. Place the heart on the wax tray with the left side to your right-hand side.
2. Examine the coronary artery running across the surface of the heart. Trace the artery up to the top of the heart and try to find where it comes from the aorta. You may need to trim some fat away carefully.
3. Identify the two atria and the two ventricles and feel the differences in the thickness of the walls.
4. Use your scissors to pierce the left atrium wall; then use them to cut down the heart in a straight line from the left atrium to the left ventricle. Your teacher will show you where to cut.
5. Open up the left atrium and the left ventricle to the apex of the heart.
6. Identify the heart strings, or tendinous cords (chordae tendinae). Observe their attachment via papillary muscles to the bicuspid valve and the ventricle wall.
7. Trace where the aorta exits the left ventricle and identify the semilunar valve at the entrance to the aorta. Use the blunt seeker to find openings and structures without cutting the tissue.

8 Measure the thickness of the walls of the left atrium and the left ventricle in several places. Record your measurements in a suitable table in the space below.

9 Continue the dissection by cutting open the right side of the heart in the same way as the left.

10 Open up the right side of the heart and measure the thickness of the atrium and ventricle walls. Identify the tricuspid valve, where the pulmonary artery exits the heart, and the semilunar valve.

11 Draw a diagram of your dissection and annotate it. Add a scale to your drawing.

12 Annotate your drawing with the measurements you have recorded.

Learning tip

The heart is twisted so that the right ventricle (to your left as you dissect the heart) spirals behind and the left ventricle spirals to the front. To open the heart, it is better to make diagonal cuts following the coronary artery, since this artery follows the internal wall between the ventricles (the septum).

Record your measurements here.

Use this space to draw your diagram.

Analysis of results

Calculate a mean value for the thickness of the heart wall you measured in step 8.

Questions

1 What do you notice about the relative sizes of the four heart chambers?

2 The left ventricle has a much thicker wall than the right ventricle. Explain why.

3 What is the function of the tendinous cords attached to the bicuspid and tricuspid valves?

....

....

....

....

4 Explain how blood flows through the heart in one direction only. Trace the movement of a single red blood cell through the heart.

....

....

....

....

....

....

....

....

....

....

....

5 What is the function of the coronary arteries?

....

....

....

....

....

....

....

....

....

....

....

....

Practical 14
Using a potometer to determine water uptake

PAG 5 11

CPAC links		Evidence	Done
2a	Correctly uses appropriate instrumentation, apparatus and materials (including ICT) to carry out investigative activities, experimental techniques and procedures with minimal assistance or prompting.	Practical procedure	
2b	Carries out techniques or procedures methodically, in sequence and in combination, identifying practical issues and making adjustments when necessary.	Practical procedure	
2c	Identifies and controls significant quantitative variables where applicable, and plans approaches to take account of variables that cannot readily be controlled.	Planning and practical procedure	
3b	Uses appropriate safety equipment and approaches to minimise risks with minimal prompting.	Practical procedure	
4b	Obtains accurate, precise and sufficient data for experimental and investigative procedures and records this methodically using appropriate units and conventions.	Practical procedure and results table	

Diagram

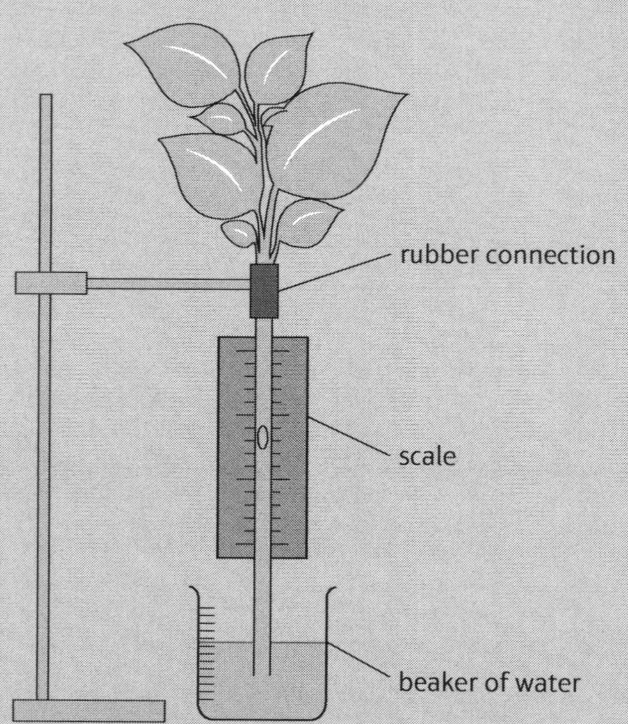

Figure A. Using a potometer to determine the water uptake of a plant

Objectives

- To determine water uptake in a leafy shoot
- To investigate the effect of environmental conditions on water uptake

Equipment

- eye protection, disposable gloves
- a large leafy shoot (with the end cut and kept under water)
- large sink
- capillary tubing (with stick-on scale) with a short rubber connecting tube attached to one end
- petroleum jelly
- a knife to trim the shoot under water
- clamp, stand
- 500 cm^3 beaker
- stop clock
- paper towels
- fan
- dark cupboard
- water baths as required
- humidifier

Safety

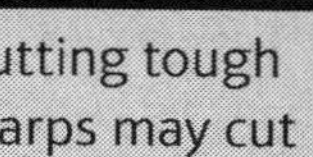

- Take care while cutting tough woody shoots; sharps may cut your skin.
- Do not use excessive force when assembling the apparatus or the glass tubing may break.
- Keep water away from electrical items, such as fans.
- Be aware that some plants may trigger allergies or skin irritation. Wash your hands after handling plant material.
- Ensure the room is well ventilated.

Procedure

Read the procedure below. Identify at least three key factors that may affect the rate of water uptake. Describe how easily these factors can be controlled in this experiment.

....

....

....

....

....

....

....

....

....

....

....

1. Lay the capillary tube and the rubber connector under water in a large sink. Fill both parts with water.
2. Carefully select a leafy shoot. The diameter of the stem should be as similar as possible to the diameter of the rubber connector. Keep the end of the shoot under water while you select it and trim it with a knife, if necessary. Make sure you do not get any water on the leaves.
3. Quickly insert the shoot into the rubber connector, making sure it fits as tightly as possible. Carry out this step under water.
4. Remove the apparatus from the water and firmly clamp the capillary tube to the stand, with the shoot at the top end (see Figure A). Place the bottom end of the capillary tube into the beaker filled with water. You may need to work with another student so the leafy shoot does not become detached.
5. Smear petroleum jelly around the point at which the shoot and the rubber connector join, to ensure an airtight seal.
6. Leave the apparatus for 5 minutes. Water will be drawn up into the end of the capillary tube, forming a small air bubble.
7. If no air bubble forms, quickly remove the tube from the water and place the open end on a paper towel. Then replace the tube in the beaker of water; a small air bubble should now be visible.
8. Time how long it takes for the air bubble to move a set distance along the capillary tube. Record this time in a suitable table.
9. 'Reset' the air bubble by repeating step 7.
10. Repeat step 8, changing the environmental conditions as instructed by your teacher. Allow the shoot to settle in the new conditions for 2–3 minutes before testing.

Learning tip

The rate of water uptake represents the rate of transpiration.

Record your results here.

Analysis of results

- Find the volume of water taken up by the shoot by multiplying the inside cross-sectional area of the tube by the distance the bubble moves.

....

....

- Calculate the rate of water uptake by dividing this volume by the time taken for the bubble to move.

....

....

- Where repeat readings are possible, calculate a mean.

....

....

Questions

1 The experiment measures the rate of water uptake. Can this be taken as equal to the rate of transpiration?

....

....

....

....

....

....

....

....

2 Why is it necessary to form an airtight seal between the shoot and the rubber tubing?

....

....

....

3 What are the limitations of this procedure?

....

....

....

....

....

....

....

4 What effect will these limitations have on your data?

5 Suggest ways of reducing these limitations to give more accurate data.

6 How could you modify the method to compare different shoots?

PAG 3

CPAC links		Evidence	Done
1a	Correctly follows instructions to carry out the experimental techniques or procedures.	Practical procedure	
2a	Correctly uses appropriate instrumentation, apparatus and materials (including ICT) to carry out investigative activities, experimental techniques and procedures with minimal assistance or prompting.	Practical procedure	
2c	Identifies and controls significant quantitative variables where applicable, and plans approaches to take account of variables that cannot be controlled.	Practical procedure and answers to questions	
4b	Obtains accurate, precise and sufficient data for experimental and investigative procedures and records this methodically using appropriate units and conventions.	Practical procedure and results table	
5a	Uses appropriate software and/ or tools to process data, carry out research and report findings.	Spreadsheet and answers to questions	

Objectives

- To determine species abundance in a specific habitat
- To investigate the effect of soil moisture content on species distribution

Equipment

- eye protection
- random number tables
- two tapes of 20 m or more with metre divisions
- one $0.5\,m^2$ quadrat per person
- identification key or sheet of illustrations for identification
- small scoop for soil collection
- recording sheet, pencil and clipboard
- clear plastic bag to protect the recording sheet from rain
- top pan balance accurate to 0.1 g
- evaporating basin
- drying oven
- desiccator
- tongs or protective gloves
- 15 small, lidded containers or small plastic bags labelled for each quadrat

Safety 

- Inform your teacher if you or other students in your group are allergic to specific plant species.
- Use tongs or protective gloves when handling hot evaporating basins.
- Cover cuts in skin with waterproof dressings.
- Wash your hands thoroughly after handling plants, animals or soil.

Diagram

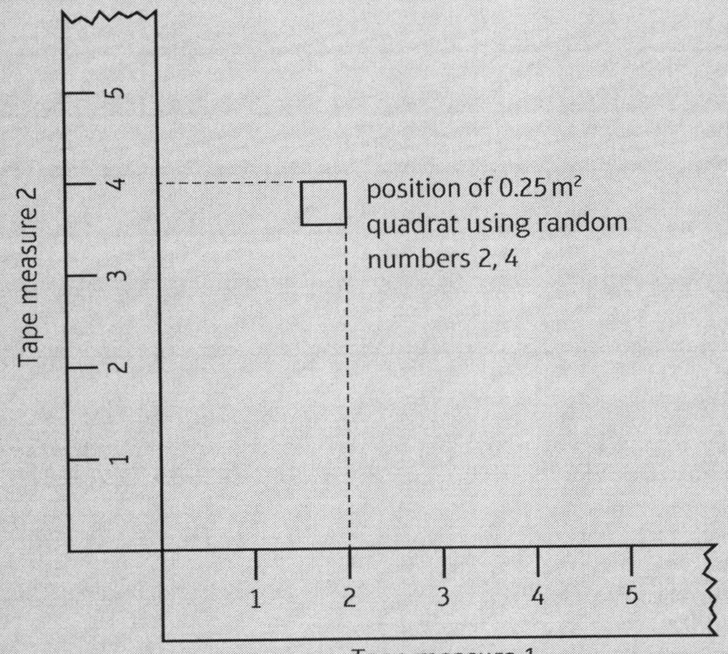

Figure A. Placing a quadrat using random numbers

Procedure

1 Go to the area indicated to you by your teacher.

2 Use the random number tables to pick 15 pairs of numbers from 1 to 20. These pairs will act as your coordinates.

3 Place the two 20 m tapes at right angles to each other across the chosen habitat, as shown in Figure A.

4 Use the first pair of numbers to place the quadrat onto the marked area. The first number gives the *x*-coordinate for the horizontal tape; the second number gives the *y*-coordinate for the vertical tape. For example, in Figure A, the numbers 2 and 4 give the coordinates 2 m along the horizontal tape and 4 m along the vertical tape. The upper right corner of the quadrat should be placed at the point where the two coordinates cross.

5 Your teacher will tell you the three dominant species most likely to be found in your chosen habitat. Count the number of each of these species present in the first quadrat.

6 Record your data in a suitable table in the space provided.

7 Use the scoop to collect a small sample of soil (approximately 15 g) from the quadrat. Place the soil sample in a small, lidded container or bag, labelled with the coordinates.

8 Repeat steps 4–7 with the remaining quadrats.

9 In the laboratory, test each soil sample for moisture content. Place each sample in an evaporating basin and weigh on a top pan balance. Record the starting mass in your results table.

10 Place in an oven at 80 °C for about 12 hours. Cool and then reweigh.

11 Repeat step 10 until a constant mass is achieved, using a desiccator between heatings to prevent atmospheric moisture affecting the sample.

12 Record the final mass in your results table.

Learning tip

The species abundance is the number of organisms of a particular species present in a chosen habitat.

Record your results here.

Analysis of results

- For each species, plot a suitable graph of moisture content against species abundance.
- Use statistical tests to decide if any trends are statistically significant. Your teacher will guide you on this.

Plot your graph here.

Plot your graph here.

Plot your graph here.

Record your processed data here (or print out the spreadsheet and stick it in here).

Questions

1 Use your data to determine the relationship between soil moisture content and the distribution of the three species you considered in your habitat.

....

....

....

....

....

2 Suggest a statistical test that would be suitable for analysing the data collected. Apply this test to your data. Your teacher will help with this. Record your processed data in the space above.

....

3 Use the results of the statistical test to comment on the accuracy of your data.

4 Comment on the validity of your own data based on your answer to question 3.

5 Apart from moisture content, suggest three other abiotic factors that may affect the distribution of the three species you have studied.

6 Why was sampling carried out using random numbers to position the quadrats?

7 Explain why standing in the middle of the area to be studied and throwing quadrats would not result in random sampling.

PAG 1

CPAC links		Evidence	Done
1a	Correctly follows instructions to carry out the experimental techniques or procedures.	Practical procedure	
2d	Selects appropriate equipment and measurement strategies in order to ensure suitably accurate results.	Measurements and magnification calculations	
4a	Makes accurate observations relevant to the experimental or investigative procedure.	Diagrams	
4b	Obtains accurate, precise and sufficient data for experimental and investigative procedures and records this methodically using appropriate units and conventions.	Measurements	

Objectives

- To investigate the distribution of tissue in the pancreas
- To make annotated diagrams of acinar cells, ducts and the islets of Langerhans

Equipment

- permanent differentially stained slides of the pancreas
- microscope with low, medium and high power objective lenses
- microscope graticule

Safety 

- Take care when handling glass slides. Do not use slides with sharp or broken edges.
- Take care when using the microscope – the lamp and lamp housing can get hot.

Procedure

1 Place a prepared slide of the pancreas on the microscope stage.

2 Move the slide carefully so the tissue is in the centre of the field of view. Using the low power objective lens and the coarse focusing knob, focus until there is a clear view of the tissue.

3 Identify the islets of Langerhans, which will be visible as patches of tissue. Between these patches are the ducts surrounded by acinar cells.

4 Draw a low power plan of the tissue distribution to show the position of the islets, ducts and acinar cells. Draw the outline of one islet only. Do not draw any cells, since this is a low power plan. Annotate your diagram fully.

5 Turn the objective disc to the medium power lens and again focus until the cells are clear.

6 Now turn the objective disc to the high power lens and refocus using the fine focusing knob only.

7 Draw five or six acinar cells around a duct. In a separate diagram, draw five or six cells of the islet tissue to show some of the different cells. Draw these cells as accurately as possible, so that they could easily be identified from the slide. Annotate both drawings fully and include a scale. Use the microscope graticule to measure the length and breadth of the cells and record these on the diagrams.

Using the microscope graticule

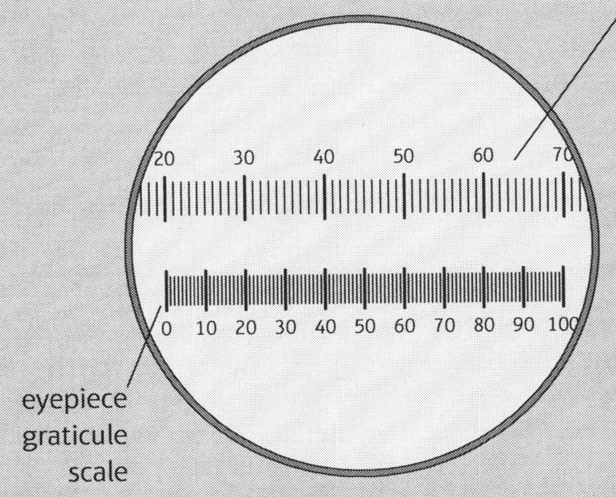

Figure A. Calibrating the stage micrometer using an eyepiece graticule

Learning tips

- Look at other micrographs of pancreas tissue to become familiar with other views. You may be given such micrographs to interpret in the exam.
- Annotating means giving greater detail about each label, which may be descriptive and can include details of size, colour and texture.

Use this space to draw your low power diagram.

Use this space to draw the cells around a duct. (Leave space to record your measurements.)

Use this space to draw cells of the islet tissue. (Leave space to record your measurements.)

Questions

1 How many different cell types did you observe in the islet tissue?

....

2 State how one visible feature of the islets of Langerhans relates to their function.

....

....

3 Use your biological knowledge to explain how each of the different cell types in islet tissue is important in the body.

....

....

....

....

4 Describe the appearance and arrangement of the acinar cells and relate this to their function.

....

....

....

....

5 Using the scale bar that you have included in your detailed drawing of cells, work out the magnification of each of your drawings.

Layout of tissues:

....

....

....

....

Cells around a duct:

....

....

....

....

Cells of the islet tissue:

....

....

....

....

PAG 1

CPAC links		Evidence	Done
1a	Correctly follows instructions to carry out the experimental techniques or procedures.	Practical procedure	
2d	Selects appropriate equipment and measurement strategies in order to ensure suitably accurate results.	Measurements and magnification calculations	
4a	Makes accurate observations relevant to the experimental or investigative procedure.	Diagrams	
4b	Obtains accurate, precise and sufficient data for experimental and investigative procedures and records this methodically using appropriate units and conventions.	Measurements	

Objectives

- To investigate the distribution of tissue in the kidney
- To make annotated diagrams of kidney tubules, Bowman's capsule and capillaries

Equipment

- permanent differentially stained slides of the kidney (transverse section)
- microscope with low, medium and high power objective lenses
- microscope graticule

Safety

- Take care when handling glass slides. Do not use slides with sharp or broken edges.
- Take care when using the microscope – the lamp and lamp housing can get hot.

Procedure

1. Place a prepared slide of the kidney on the microscope stage.
2. Move the slide carefully so the tissue is in the centre of the field of view. Using the low power objective lens and the coarse focusing knob, focus until there is a clear view of the tissue.
3. Identify the Bowman's capsule in the kidney cortex. Within the capsule is the knot of capillaries called the glomerulus.
4. Draw a low power plan of the tissue distribution to show the position of the Bowman's capsule, kidney tubules and glomerulus. Annotate your diagram. Do not draw any cells, since this is a low power plan.
5. Turn the objective lens to medium power and refocus until the cells are clearly visible.
6. Now turn the objective disc to the high power lens and refocus using the fine focusing knob only.
7. Draw 10–15 cells to show the Bowman's capsule wall and glomerular cells, and annotate the diagram. Draw these cells as accurately as possible, so that they could easily be identified from the slide. Include a scale on the diagram.
8. Use the microscope graticule to measure the diameter of the Bowman's capsule cup and of the glomerulus within it.
9. Move the slide to the medulla tissue and repeat step 7 to draw the cells of the loop of Henle and tubules of the medulla.

Using the microscope graticule

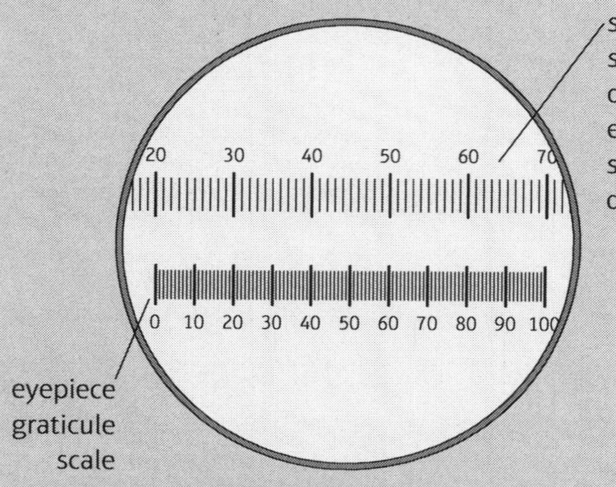

Figure A. Calibrating the stage micrometer using an eyepiece graticule

Learning tips

- Look at other micrographs of kidney tissue to become familiar with other views. You may be given such micrographs to interpret in the exam.
- Try to relate what you see under the microscope to the theory of how the nephron works.

Use this space to draw your low power diagram.

Use this space to draw the cells showing the Bowman's capsule wall and glomerular cells.
(Leave space to record your measurements.)

Use this space to draw the cells of the loop of Henle and tubules of the medulla.
(Leave space to record your measurements.)

Questions

1 Describe the appearance of the cells making up the Bowman's capsule in the kidney cortex.

2 Use your biological knowledge to explain how the structure of the capsule is related to its function of ultrafiltration.

3 Describe the part the glomerulus plays in ultrafiltration.

4 Describe and explain the difference in the tissue distribution of the kidney cortex and the kidney medulla.

PAG 1

CPAC links		Evidence	Done
2a	Correctly uses appropriate instrumentation, apparatus and materials (including ICT) to carry out investigative activities, experimental techniques and procedures with minimal assistance or prompting.	Practical procedure	
2d	Selects appropriate equipment and measurement strategies in order to ensure suitably accurate results.	Measurements and magnification calculations	
4a	Makes accurate observations relevant to the experimental or investigative procedure.	Diagrams	
4b	Obtains accurate, precise and sufficient data for experimental and investigative procedures and records this methodically using appropriate units and conventions.	Measurements	

Objectives

- To investigate the structure of muscle tissue
- To make annotated diagrams of muscle tissue

Equipment

- permanent differentially stained slides of skeletal/striated muscle (longitudinal section)
- microscope with low, medium and high power objective lenses
- microscope graticule

Safety 

- Take care when handling glass slides. Do not use slides with sharp or broken edges.
- Take care when using the microscope – the lamp and lamp housing can get hot.

Procedure

1. Place a prepared slide of skeletal muscle on the microscope stage.
2. Move the slide carefully so the tissue is in the centre of the field of view. Using the low power objective lens and the coarse focusing knob, focus until there is a clear view of the tissue.
3. Identify individual muscle fibres, nuclei and glycogen granules.
4. Draw a low power plan of at least three muscle fibres to show how they are arranged. Annotate your diagram. Include nuclei but do not draw any other cellular detail since this is a low power plan.
5. Turn the objective lens to medium power and refocus until the cells are clearly visible.
6. Now turn the objective disc to the high power lens and refocus using the fine focusing knob only.
7. Draw a single fibre or part of a fibre to show the light (I) and dark (A) bands. If visible, include the Z lines within the light bands and try to label a sarcomere. Draw these features as accurately as possible, so that they could be easily identified from the slide.
8. Use the graticule to measure the width of a muscle fibre and a nucleus. Include a scale on the diagram.

Using the microscope graticule

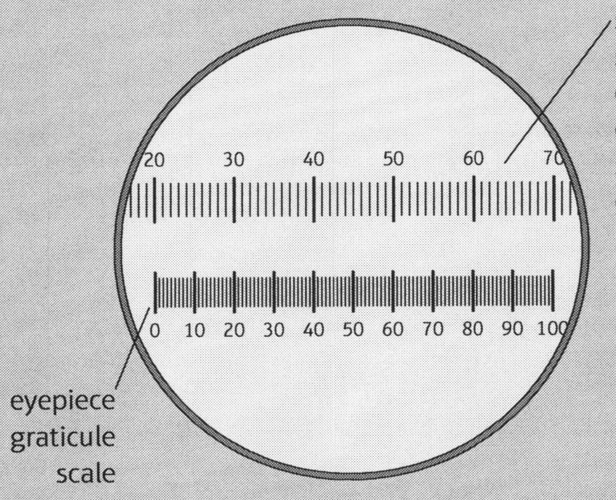

Figure A. Calibrating the stage micrometer using an eyepiece graticule

Learning tips

- Look at electron micrographs of skeletal muscle tissue to become familiar with other views. You may be given such micrographs to label and interpret in the exam.
- Try to relate what you see under the microscope and in electron micrographs to the sliding filament hypothesis of muscle contraction.

Use this space to draw your low power diagram.

Use this space to draw the fibre. (Leave space to record your measurements.)

Questions

1 Muscle cells are multinucleate. Explain what this means.

2 Why is muscle tissue arranged in long fibres?

3 How does the structure of skeletal muscle differ from that of cardiac (heart) muscle?

4 Using the scale bar that you have included in your detailed drawing of a muscle fibre, work out the magnificatior of your drawing.

PAG 9

CPAC links		Evidence	Done
1a	Correctly follows instructions to carry out the experimental techniques or procedures.	Practical procedure	
2a	Correctly uses appropriate instrumentation, apparatus and materials (including ICT) to carry out investigative activities, experimental techniques and procedures with minimal assistance or prompting.	Practical procedure	
2c	Identifies and controls significant quantitative variables where applicable, and plans approaches to take account of variables that cannot be controlled.	Practical procedure	
4a	Makes accurate observations relevant to the experimental or investigative procedure.	Observations and answers to questions	
5a	Uses appropriate software and/or tools to process data, carry out research and report findings.	Research	

Objectives

- To determine glucose concentration using a biosensor
- To investigate diabetes by determining glucose concentration in mock urine samples

Equipment

- five 5 cm^3 samples of mock urine labelled 1–5
- five small beakers or five test tubes and test tube rack
- labels or chinagraph pencil
- two micropipettes
- six strips of filter paper
- 5 cm^3 sucrose solution
- 0.1 cm^3 enzyme A
- 0.1 cm^3 indicator solution B
- hairdryer
- stop clock

Diagram

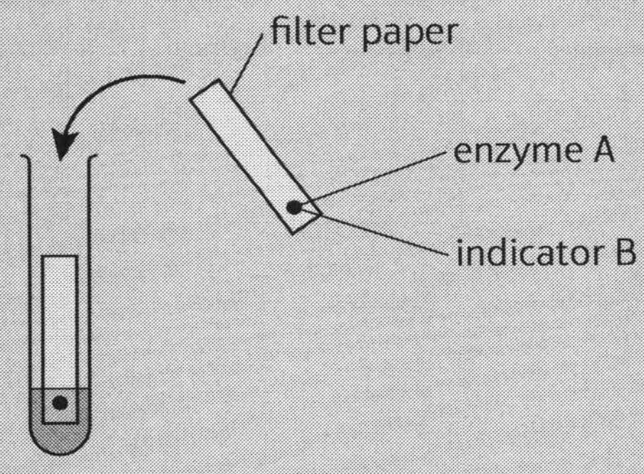

Procedure

1. Place 5 cm^3 of each unknown mock urine sample into a small beaker or test tube. Label the samples from 1 to 5.
2. Label the strips of filter paper from 1 to 6.
3. Remove 0.01 cm^3 of enzyme A using a micropipette and drop it onto the end of filter paper 1.
4. Leave it for 5 minutes until it is completely dry or use a hairdryer to hasten drying.
5. Use a clean micropipette tip and add 0.01 cm^3 of indicator B onto the dried spot.
6. Allow it to dry or again use the hairdryer. The filter paper is now your biosensor.
7. Dip the treated end of the biosensor into the mock urine sample 1 for 30 seconds.
8. Repeat steps 3–7 for each of the unknown mock urine solutions 2–5.
9. Finally, treat filter paper 6 with enzyme A and indicator B and dip it into the sucrose solution.
10. Observe the colour of each sample and record your observations in an appropriate table.

Learning tips

- Excess glucose in urine is an indicator of diabetes mellitus. You could use this opportunity to find out more about type 1 and type 2 diabetes.
- These biosensors use enzymes to test the presence of glucose quantitatively. Find out about other biosensors.

Notes from research.

Remember to cite the sources of information.

Record your results here.

Questions

1 Which sample might indicate that a patient has diabetes? How did you determine this?

2 Suggest why reagents A and B cannot be applied together.

3 What is the purpose of using a sixth test on sucrose solution?

PAG 4

CPAC links		Evidence	Done
1a	Correctly follows instructions to carry out the experimental techniques or procedures.	Practical procedure	
2b	Carries out techniques or procedures methodically, in sequence and in combination, identifying practical issues and making adjustments when necessary.	Practical procedure, answers to questions on limitations	
2c	Identifies and controls significant quantitative variables where applicable, and plans approaches to take account of variables that cannot readily be controlled.	Practical procedure and answers to questions	
4a	Makes accurate observations relevant to the experimental or investigative procedure.	Observations and answers to questions	
4b	Obtains accurate, precise and sufficient data for experimental and investigative procedures and records this methodically using appropriate units and conventions.	Results table and analysis	

Objectives

- To investigate the effect of immobilised pectinase on apple pulp
- To investigate a batch process using an immobilised enzyme

Equipment

- 2 cm^3 50% pectinase solution
- 8 cm^3 2% sodium alginate solution
- 50 cm^3 2% calcium chloride solution
- 100 cm^3 apple pulp in a boiling tube or small beaker
- four filter papers and two funnels
- 25 cm^3 measuring cylinder
- 10 cm^3 syringe
- two 5 cm^3 syringes
- one 25 cm^3 and one 50 cm^3 beaker
- glass rod
- distilled/deionised water
- stop clock

Safety

- Calcium chloride is an irritant.
- If you have any hand wounds or skin conditions, wear gloves when handling solutions.
- Wear eye protection when handling solutions.

Irritant

Diagram

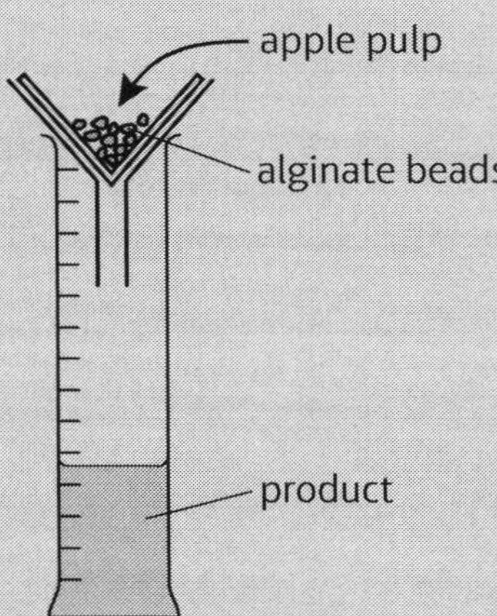

Procedure

1. Use one of the 5 cm^3 syringes to measure 8 cm^3 sodium alginate into the small beaker and use the second syringe to add 2 cm^3 pectinase enzyme. Mix with the glass rod. Use the 10 cm^3 syringe to draw up this mixture.
2. Place all the calcium chloride solution into a second beaker and add drops of the sodium alginate and pectinase mixture to the calcium chloride. Do not add the drops too quickly or make the drops too large – it is important to control the size of the drops and keep them as consistent as possible.
3. These drops will immediately form alginate beads containing the enzyme. Leave to harden for 15 minutes.

4 Strain the beads using a funnel and filter paper and rinse with distilled water over the sink. These beads are now ready to use.

5 Place the second funnel and filter paper over the measuring cylinder and add the alginate beads.

6 Pour 20 cm^3 apple pulp over the beads and leave for 10 minutes.

7 Allow the products to drain into the measuring cylinder. Record the volume of juice collected (the 'product'). This is batch 1.

8 Rinse the beads with distilled water and reuse the beads by adding more apple pulp. Record the new volume of juice. Repeat this at least twice, using a new filter paper each time.

9 Tabulate the volume of juice collected for each batch.

Learning tips

- Pectinase breaks down pectins in plant cell walls into shorter chains, which no longer hold the cell wall together. This causes any juice contained in the cells to be released.
- Immobilised enzymes are attached to inert insoluble material, which allows them to be reused. This has a commercial benefit, because it means costs can be reduced.

Record your results here.

Analysis of results

Draw a graph of your results.

Plot your graph here.

Questions

1 Explain what has happened to the enzyme activity over several batches.

2 What variables should be controlled in this experiment to obtain accurate and reliable data?

3 What are the main limitations of this technique? Where possible, suggest an improvement for each limitation given.

4 What are the main advantages of using immobilised enzymes commercially, other than cost?

PAG 4

CPAC links		Evidence	Done
1a	Correctly follows instructions to carry out the experimental techniques or procedures.	Practical procedure	
2b	Carries out techniques or procedures methodically, in sequence and in combination, identifying practical issues and making adjustments when necessary.	Practical procedure	
4a	Makes accurate observations relevant to the experimental or investigative procedure.	Observations in results table	
5a	Uses appropriate software and/or tools to process data, carry out research and report findings.	Research done	

Diagram

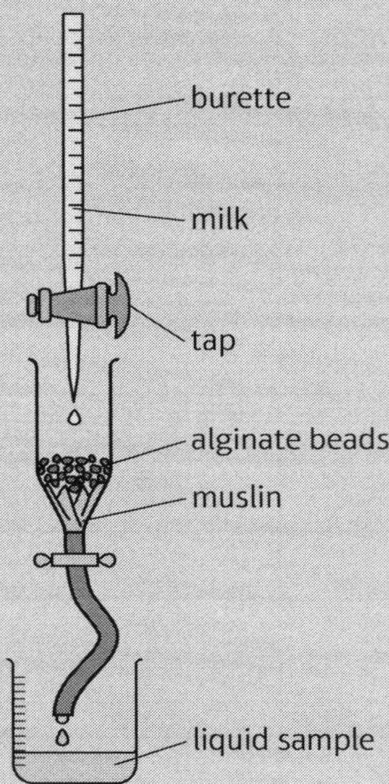

Procedure

1 Using different 5 cm^3 syringes, place 8 cm^3 sodium alginate into a small beaker and add 2 cm^3 lipase enzyme. Mix with the glass rod and draw up using the 10 cm^3 syringe.

2 Place all the calcium chloride solution into a second beaker and add drops of the sodium alginate and lipase mixture to the calcium chloride using the 10 cm^3 syringe. Add the drops slowly and keep the size of the drops as consistent as possible.

3 Alginate beads containing the enzyme will immediately form. Leave to harden for 15 minutes.

4 Strain off the beads using a strainer and rinse with distilled water. These beads are now ready to use.

Objectives

- To investigate the action of immobilised lipase on milk
- To investigate a continuous process using immobilised enzymes and compare it with a batch process (see Practical 20)

Equipment

- 30 cm^3 milk mixed with 1.5 cm^3 of 1 $mol\,dm^{-3}$ sodium hydroxide
- 2 cm^3 lipase
- 8 cm^3 2% sodium alginate solution
- 25 cm^3 2% calcium chloride solution
- tea strainer
- glass rod
- 10 cm^3 syringe
- two 5 cm^3 syringes
- 20 cm^3 syringe with short connector tube
- 50 ml burette
- retort stand, two clamps
- small piece of muslin
- two 25 cm^3 beakers
- small beaker
- distilled/deionised water
- pH meter or pH paper
- stop clock

Safety

- Calcium chloride is an irritant.
- Wear eye protection, gloves if you have any hand wounds or skin conditions, and a lab coat when using solutions.

Irritant

5 Remove the plunger from the 20 cm^3 syringe. Place a small piece of muslin inside to cover the outlet, then place the alginate beads inside.

6 Clamp the syringe into a retort stand with the outlet pointing down.

7 Pour all of the milk mixture into the burette and clamp it to the retort stand above the syringe so that when the tap is open the milk will flow into the top of the syringe.

8 Open the tap just enough to allow the milk mixture to drip slowly but continuously into the syringe.

9 Once the liquid starts to drip from the connector tube of the syringe, collect a small sample (approximately 2 cm^3). Test the pH of this product using a pH meter or pH paper.

10 Start the stop clock. Every minute for 10 minutes take a repeat sample and test its pH. If necessary, top up the milk in the burette. Record all your data in a suitable table.

Learning tips

- Immobilising enzymes allows them to be reused. Commercially, this is beneficial because it reduces costs and enzymes can be used in batch or continuous processes. Immobilised enzymes are also more stable.
- A packed bed reactor is used in continuous processes, allowing a continuous stream of product. The reactor does not need to be cleaned between batches.

Record your results here.

Analysis of results

Draw a graph of your results showing pH against time.

Plot your graph here.

Questions

1 Use your graph to compare the pH for successive samples.

2 Temperature would normally be controlled in enzyme-catalysed reactions but has not been specifically controlled in this investigation. Explain why temperature would usually be carefully controlled and suggest how this could be done.

3 Practical 20 is an example of a batch process. This practical shows how a continuous process works. Suggest which method would be best for commercial production of a product. Give reasons for your answer.

4 A student decided that immobilised enzymes could be reused without being denatured or damaged. Comment on the validity of this conclusion.

5 Research some of the commercial uses of immobilised enzymes. Remember to cite your sources.

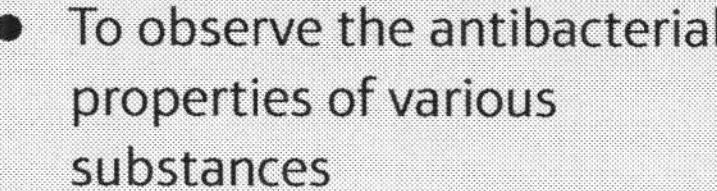

PAG 7

CPAC links		Evidence	Done
1a	Correctly follows instructions to carry out the experimental techniques or procedures.	Practical procedure	
3b	Uses appropriate safety equipment and approaches to minimise risks with minimal prompting.	Practical procedure	
4a	Makes accurate observations relevant to the experimental or investigative procedure.	Observations and answers to questions	

Diagram

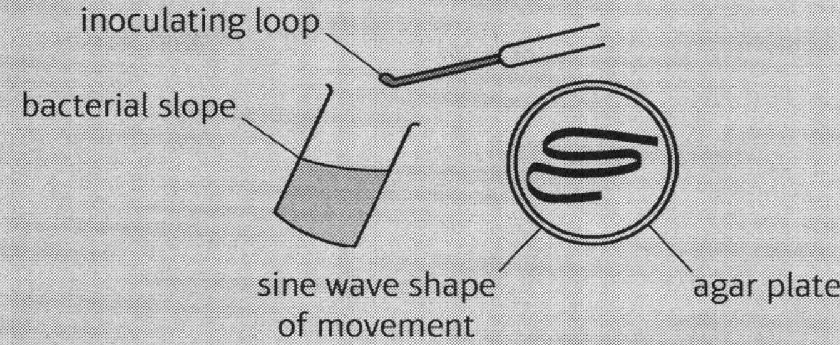

Figure A. Streaking the inoculum across the surface of the agar

Procedure

1. You will be provided with five sterile plates of agar.
2. Using aseptic techniques, carefully flame an inoculation loop or remove one from a sterile pack. Slide the cool sterile inoculation loop lightly across the surface of the bacterial slope to pick up several colonies of *Bacillus subtilis*. Inoculate each of the five agar plates by sweeping the inoculation loop across the agar in each Petri dish in the shape of a sine wave, as demonstrated by your teacher.
3. Take 5 cm^3 fresh lemon juice. Set aside 1 cm^3 of the juice and use the remainder to make dilutions using the sterile water, 10 cm^3 syringe and test tubes. Use the table below as a guide. The concentrations should provide a range from full strength (100%) down to 0% concentration.

Concentration of lemon juice (%)	Volume of water (cm^3)	Volume of lemon juice (cm^3)
100	0.0	1.0
80	0.2	0.8
60	0.4	0.6
40	0.6	0.4
20	0.8	0.2
0	1.0	0.0

4. Label the base of each dish carefully with the concentration of lemon juice to be added.
5. Flood each of the labelled, inoculated Petri dishes with 1 cm^3 of the appropriate lemon juice concentration, using a clean syringe each time.
6. Tape the lid to the Petri dish base using four strips of tape. Do not completely seal the Petri dishes.

Objectives

- To observe the antibacterial properties of various substances
- To understand the aseptic techniques required in microbial tasks

Equipment

- five agar Petri dishes
- inoculating loop
- agar slope of *Bacillus subtilis*
- chinagraph pencil, marker pen or labels
- 5 cm^3 fresh lemon juice in a small container
- five 1 cm^3 syringes
- sterile water
- tape (biohazard or other)
- incubator at 30 °C
- Bunsen burner and heat-proof mat
- six test tubes or volumetric flasks for lemon juice dilutions
- 10 cm^3 syringe

Safety

- Aseptic techniques must be followed.
- Wash hands before and after handling the apparatus.
- Disinfect the bench with 1% Virkon or equivalent. Leave the disinfectant on the bench for about 10 minutes. This should be done before and after working.
- Wear a lab coat, eye protection and disposable gloves.

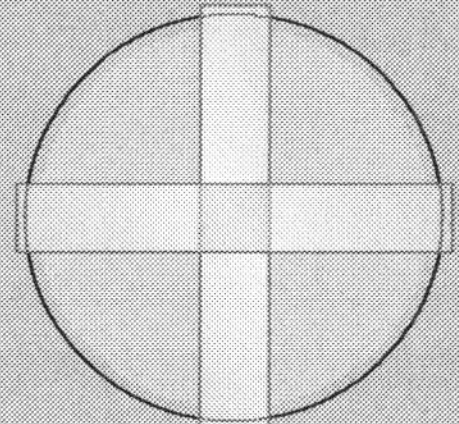

Figure B. Use adhesive tape to hold the lid on each Petri dish

7 Place all the dishes in an incubator at 30 °C for two days.

8 Observe the bacterial growth in each Petri dish.

Learning tips

- Aseptic techniques are vital to avoid contamination of the plates.
- Aseptic techniques may be examined.

Analysis of results

- For this practical, make qualitative observations of the bacterial growth. Which plates show most growth? What does the growth look like? Do these observations seem to have a relationship with lemon juice concentration?
- Try to give a subjective estimate of how much of each plate is covered by bacterial growth (for example, a percentage estimate). Your teacher can provide you with sample data. How do your findings compare with the sample data? To calculate percentage coverage for the sample data, assume that the Petri dish used had an area of 5000 mm^2.

Use this space to record your observations and estimates.

Questions

1. What differences in bacterial growth did you observe in the five Petri dishes?

....

....

....

....

....

....

....

2. How would you measure the differences in bacterial growth to acquire quantitative data from these dishes?

....

....

....

....

....

....

....

....

....

....

....

....

....

3. Use the data provided in the table below to draw a suitable graph representing the growth of bacteria in each dilution of lemon juice.

Concentration of lemon juice (%)	**Area of bacterial growth (mm^2)**
100	97
80	125
60	140
40	253
20	418

Plot your graph here.

PAG 4 | 5 | 9 | 11

CPAC links		Evidence	Done
1a	Correctly follows instructions to carry out the experimental techniques or procedures.	Practical procedure	
2b	Carries out techniques or procedures methodically, in sequence and in combination, identifying practical issues and making adjustments when necessary.	Practical procedure, answers to question on limitations	
4a	Makes accurate observations relevant to the experimental or investigative procedure.	Observations and answers to questions	

Objectives

- To investigate the effect of temperature on cellular membranes
- To determine from this some properties of membranes

Equipment

- eye protection, lab coat, disposable gloves
- water baths, pre-set to the required temperatures
- thermometer
- distilled water buffered to pH 7
- large beetroot (one per student)
- cork borer size no. 5
- ruler
- white tile
- knife
- syringe
- pipettes
- test tubes
- colorimeter
- cuvettes
- labels
- waterproof marker pen
- forceps
- stop clock
- paper towels

Safety

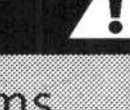

- Take care with sharp items such as cork borers and knives.
- Take care with hot water in baths above 40 °C.
- Avoid direct contact between water and the electrical components of, for example, water baths and colorimeters.

Diagrams

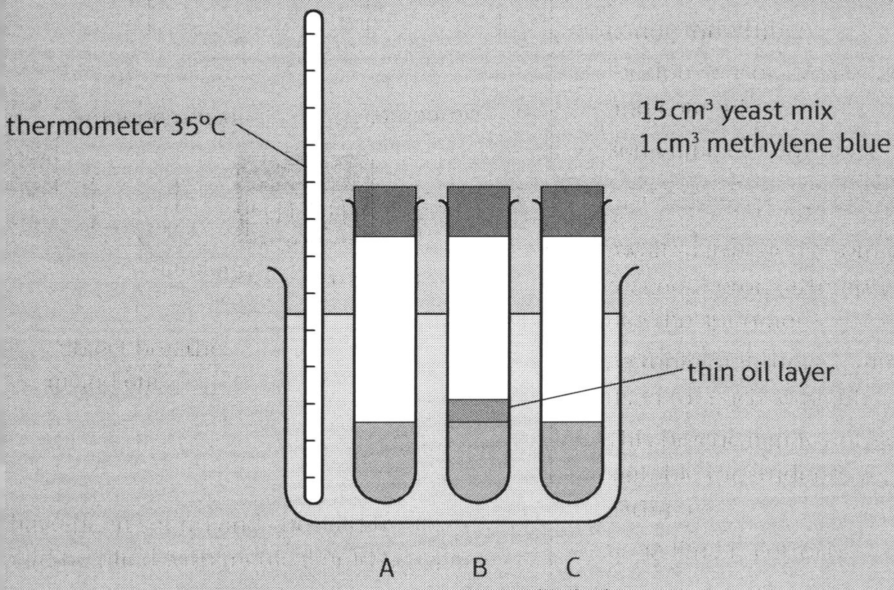

Figure A. Experimental set-up

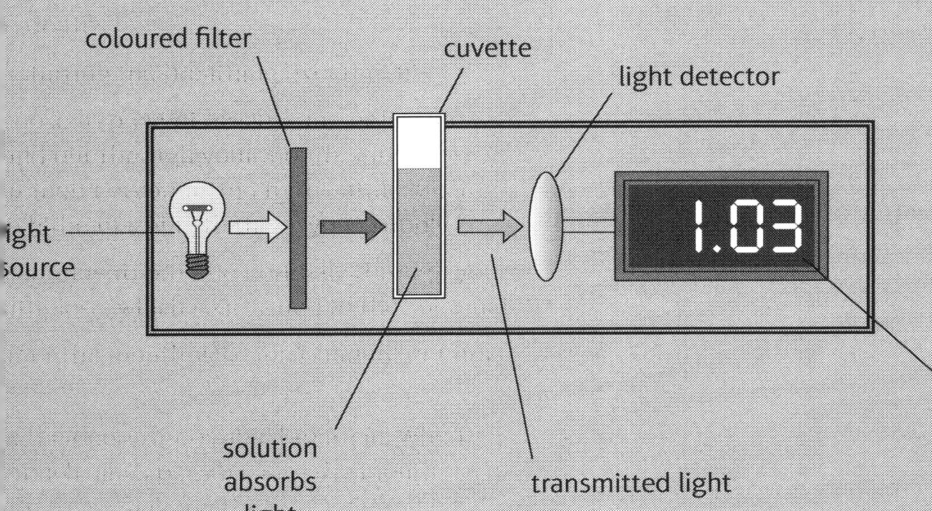

Figure B. Using a colorimeter

Procedure

1 Set up two water baths: one with boiling water and one with water at 35 °C.

2 Label three boiling tubes A, B and C. Stir the yeast mixture and add 15 cm^3 to each tube using the larger syringe.

3 Put tube C into the boiling water bath and boil for 5 minutes. Remove tube C and cool under cold running water. This is your control.

4 Place all three tubes into the second water bath at 35 °C. Check the temperature with a thermometer regularly throughout the following steps.

5 Add 1 cm^3 of methylene blue to each of the three tubes using the small syringe. Cover each tube using the metal foil or rubber bungs.

6 Gently shake each tube until the blue colour is evenly distributed.

7 Add a thin layer of oil to tube B and re-cover.

8 Leave all three tubes in the water bath for 10 minutes.

9 Remove the tubes, taking care not to shake them, and record your observations in a suitable table.

10 Fill three colorimeter tubes with samples from each boiling tube and measure the absorbance for each sample. You may need to dilute the samples to achieve 0% absorbance for control tube C containing the boiled yeast solution.

Learning tips

- A redox reaction is one where one substance is *red*uced and another *ox*idised. This is a good opportunity to remind yourself of this concept.
- A colorimeter measures the amount of light that is absorbed by a coloured liquid. As the liquid becomes darker, the amount of light absorbed increases. This is called the absorbance. You should be familiar with how a colorimeter works from the first year of your A level study.
- The action of dehydrogenase enzymes can be detected using methylene blue as an artificial hydrogen acceptor. Methylene blue can readily be reduced to a colourless form and re-oxidised back into the blue-coloured form.

(*oxidised*) (*reduced*)
coloured methylene blue ⟶ colourless methylene blue

Record your results here.

Analysis of results

If you have used a colorimeter, you can plot your results on a bar chart.

Plot your graph here.

Questions

1 What is the purpose of the oil in tube B?

....

....

2 Describe and explain the difference in your observations for tubes A, B and C after leaving them for 10 minutes in the water bath.

....

....

....

....

....

....

....

....

....

3 Describe three limitations to this method and suggest an improvement for each.

....

....

....

....

....

....

....

....

....

4 Use your biological knowledge to explain what happens to the hydrogen in living cells when methylene blue is not present.

....

....

....

5 What is the advantage of using colorimeter readings for a reaction such as this?

....

....

PAG 4 | 11 | 12

CPAC links		Evidence	Done
1a	Correctly follows instructions to carry out the experimental techniques or procedures.	Practical procedure	
2b	Carries out techniques or procedures methodically, in sequence and in combination, identifying practical issues and making adjustments when necessary.	Practical procedure, answers to questions	
2d	Selects appropriate equipment and measurement strategies in order to ensure suitably accurate results.	Practical procedure, answers to questions	
4a	Makes accurate observations relevant to the experimental or investigative procedure.	Observations and results table	
4b	Obtains accurate, precise and sufficient data for experimental and investigative procedures and records this methodically using appropriate units and conventions.	Observations and results table	
5a	Uses appropriate software and/or tools to process data, carry out research and report findings.	Research done	
5b	Sources of information are cited, demonstrating that research has taken place, supporting planning and conclusions.	Report with citations	

Objectives

- To investigate the effect of different substrates on yeast respiration
- To conduct individual research into methods for measuring rate of respiration and the effect of different substrates on respiration

Equipment

- water bath at 40 °C or beaker with warm water
- thermometer
- four boiling tubes
- four Durham tubes
- pencil with rubber end
- four 2 cm^3 yeast solutions, one for each substrate used
- 2 cm^3 glucose solution
- 2 cm^3 fructose solution
- 2 cm^3 maltose solution
- 2 cm^3 sucrose solution
- stop clock
- ruler
- chinagraph pencil

Safety

- If a kettle is used to heat water, take care with hot water.

Diagram

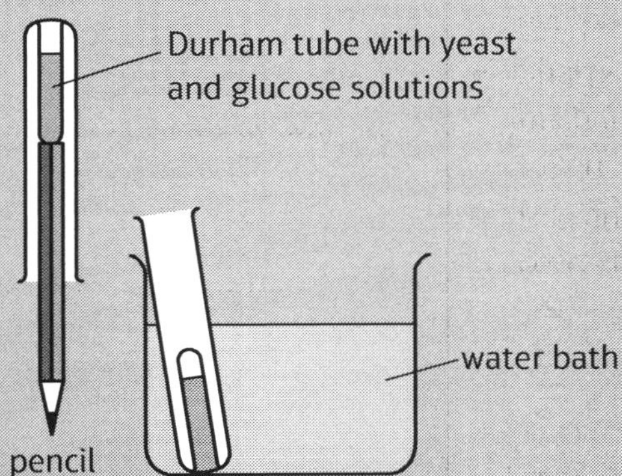

Figure A. Push the fluid-filled smaller tube to the end of a boiling tube and invert

Procedure

1. Assemble the apparatus as shown in the diagram. Partly fill the beaker with warm water or use a water bath that has already been set up.
2. Place 2 cm^3 yeast solution and 2 cm^3 glucose solution in a Durham tube and cover with a boiling tube. Use the rubber end of a pencil to hold the Durham tube firmly in place and then carefully invert the boiling tube. Ensure that none of the mixture escapes.

3. Place the apparatus into the water bath and wait for the yeast to start respiring. When bubbles begin to appear in the Durham tube, start the stop clock.
4. Wait for 3 minutes and then use the ruler to measure and record the height of the gas produced in the Durham tube.
5. Take the apparatus apart and reassemble, this time using another substrate (fructose, maltose or sucrose) in place of the glucose.
6. Repeat steps 3–5 for each substrate, recording the height of gas produced each time.
7. Consider how you could modify the apparatus to roughly measure the volume of gas produced. Discuss with other students and your teacher. Once agreed with your teacher, write out the extra procedure steps required. Repeat the experiment using this modification. Work out the rate of respiration with the most active substrate.

Learning tips

- Yeast is a single-celled fungus that feeds on rotting fruit and other carbohydrates.
- Yeast decomposes carbohydrates using either anaerobic fermentation or aerobic respiration.
- Complex carbohydrates are converted to glucose before being used in respiration.
- Remember: all respiration involves specific enzymes for specific substrates.
- Always follow a recognised format for citing references from scientific journals. Do not include the web address alone, even if sources are available online.

Record your results here.

rite the extra procedure steps and calculated rate of respiration here.

nalysis of results

lot a suitable graph to show the height of gas produced against the different substrates.

Plot your graph here.

Questions

To answer questions 1–3, conduct some individual research online and in textbooks. Use this research to explain your findings in a report and reference your sources using a recognised format such as the Harvard system. Your teacher will brief you on this.

1. How accurate and precise are these results? Suggest improvements that would give greater accuracy and precision.

2. Which substrate showed the highest rate of respiration? Explain this result using your own research and your knowledge of respiration.

3. A student carried out this experiment with lactose as the respiratory substrate. No gas was obtained after 10 minutes. What is the most likely biological explanation for this result?

Write your notes on your research and citations for preparing your report here.

PAG 4 | 11

CPAC links		Evidence	Done
1a	Correctly follows instructions to carry out the experimental techniques or procedures.	Practical procedure	
2c	Identifies and controls significant quantitative variables where applicable, and plans approaches to take account of variables that cannot readily be controlled.	Practical procedure, answers to questions	
4b	Obtains accurate, precise and sufficient data for experimental and investigative procedures and records this methodically using appropriate units and conventions.	Observations and results table	
5a	Uses appropriate software and/or tools to process data, carry out research and report findings.	Spreadsheet and graph	

Objective

- To investigate the effect of carbon dioxide as a limiting factor in photosynthesis

Equipment

- young cabbage leaf or similar, such as spinach or ivy (*Hedera*)
- cork borer or straw
- 5 cm^3 syringe
- modelling clay
- 5 cm^3 each of four different concentrations of sodium hydrogencarbonate solution (0.0 $mol\,dm^{-3}$, 0.2 $mol\,dm^{-3}$, 0.4 $mol\,dm^{-3}$ and 0.6 $mol\,dm^{-3}$)
- bench lamp with 40 W bulb
- stop clock

Safety 

- Take care with sharp cork borers.
- The electric lamp should not come into contact with water or other liquids, including water on wet hands.

Diagram

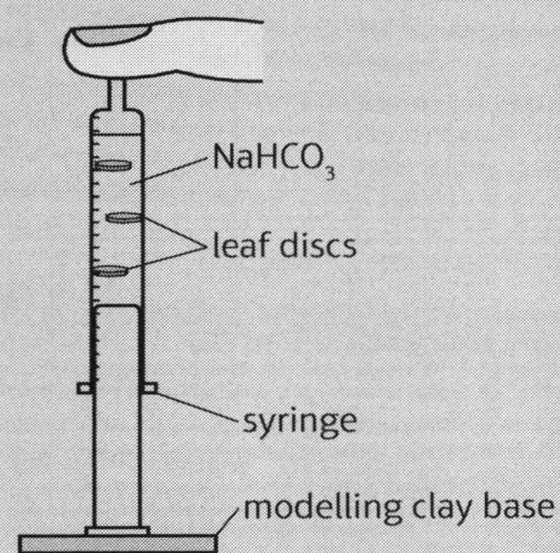

Procedure

1. Cut out 20 leaf discs from the cabbage leaves using a cork borer or straw.
2. Remove the plunger from the syringe. Place a finger over the nozzle to prevent liquid running out, then fill with 5 cm^3 of 0.2 $mol\,dm^{-3}$ sodium hydrogencarbonate solution.
3. Carefully add five of the leaf discs to the solution in the syringe, taking care not to damage them.
4. Gently replace the syringe plunger and point the syringe upwards.
5. Push out all the air by slowly pushing the plunger until all of the air has been expelled.
6. Place your finger over the syringe nozzle and gradually pull the plunger down. Bubbles will appear on the surface of the leaf discs as the air is drawn out of them.
7. Tap the syringe barrel so that the bubbles rise to the top and the discs start to sink to the bottom.
8. Repeat this process until all the discs are at the bottom of the syringe.

9 Use a piece of modelling clay to hold the syringe barrel vertically under a bench lamp with the nozzle pointing up. Start the stop clock and time how long it takes for each disc to rise to the surface.

10 Repeat steps 2–9 for each concentration of sodium hydrogencarbonate.

11 Record your times in a suitable table.

Learning tips

- The rate of a metabolic process that depends on a number of factors is limited by the factor that is present at its least favourable (lowest) level. This is the limiting factor.
- Where there are several factors that affect photosynthesis, the one that is at its lowest level will determine (or limit) the rate of photosynthesis.
- Sodium hydrogencarbonate is a source of CO_2.

Record your results here.

Analysis of results

- Convert timings in minutes and seconds into results in either minutes or seconds. Calculate means for your groups of five discs and plot a graph of your results.
- Calculate the reciprocal of your mean times $\left(\frac{1}{T}\right)$ and plot this on another graph. You will need to adjust the scales.
- The overall shape of the curve will be the same but inverted and more directly comparable to standard rate and limiting factor curves seen in textbooks and exam questions.

Record your processed data and make calculations here (or print out the spreadsheet and stick it in here).

Plot your graphs here.

Analysis of graph

Explain the shape of your graph, relating it to the idea of limiting factors.

Questions

1 Why did the discs rise to the surface of the syringe?

2 What assumptions were made about the gas bubbles? Evaluate the validity of these assumptions.

Explain the difference in rate of photosynthesis between the different sodium hydrogencarbonate solutions.

What other factors may affect photosynthesis and so affect your results?

How did you try to minimise the effect of other factors that could limit the rate of photosynthesis?

How could a horticulturist use information about limiting factors when growing a crop in a greenhouse?

Practical 26 Investigate the effect of changing light intensity on the photosynthesis rate of *Cabomba*

PAG 4 | 11

CPAC links		Evidence	Done
2b	Carries out techniques or procedures methodically, in sequence and in combination, identifying practical issues and making adjustments when necessary.	Practical procedure	
2c	Identifies and controls significant quantitative variables where applicable, and plans approaches to take account of variables that cannot readily be controlled.	Practical procedure and answers to questions	
4b	Obtains accurate, precise and sufficient data for experimental and investigative procedures and records this methodically using appropriate units and conventions.	Observations and results table	
5a	Uses appropriate software and/or tools to process data, carry out research and report findings.	Spreadsheet and graph	

Objective

- To determine the effect of light intensity as a limiting factor on the rate of photosynthesis

Equipment

- piece of *Cabomba* approximately 10 cm long
- large beaker covered in black paper with a single vertical light slit
- potassium hydrogencarbonate
- thermometer
- spatula
- photosynthometer (Audus microburette) or similar apparatus with a scale
- boiling tube
- bench lamp
- ruler
- stop clock
- coloured dye (optional)

Safety

- Take care to keep the electric lamp away from water.

Diagram

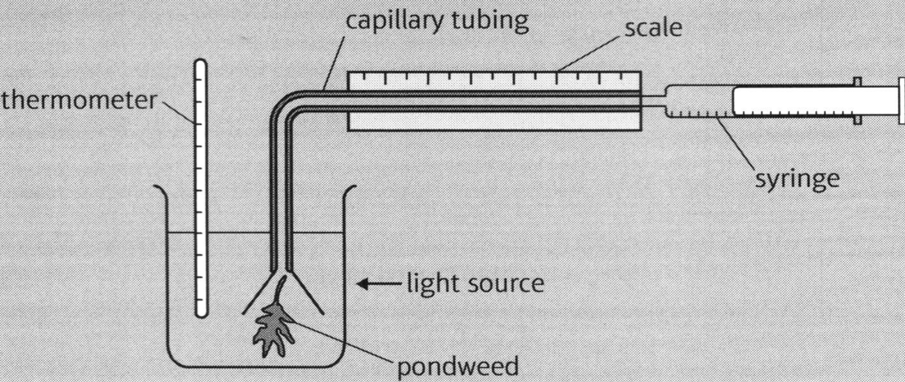

Procedure

1. Place a piece of *Cabomba*, approximately 10 cm long, into a large beaker of water covered in black paper with a vertical slit. Position the *Cabomba* with the cut end at the top and use a thermometer to make sure the water remains close to 20 °C throughout the experiment. Add more cold water when necessary. Remove any bubbles on the surface of the *Cabomba* by gently running a finger and thumb over the surface of the *Cabomba* under the water.
2. Add a spatula of potassium hydrogencarbonate to the water and leave for 5 minutes.
3. Fill the capillary tubing of the photosynthometer (Audus microburette) with water. Coloured dye can be added to make it easier to see the bubble and read the distance travelled.
4. Place the funnel end of the tubing into the beaker of water.
5. Position the bench lamp approximately 10 cm away from the beaker and allow the *Cabomba* to adjust for 5 minutes.

Fix the cut end of the *Cabomba* into the funnel opening of the apparatus. Start the stop clock.

After 2 minutes gently pull the syringe plunger and bring the oxygen bubble into the tube against the scale. Read the length of the bubble and use this measurement to record the volume of gas produced.

Move the lamp to 15 cm away from the beaker and leave for 5 minutes. Check that the temperature of the water remains constant and refill the capillary tube.

Start the stop clock again and record the volume of gas produced in 2 minutes.

0 Repeat steps 7–9 three more times, moving the lamp to a new distance each time.

1 Tabulate your results.

earning tips

- Light intensity is proportional to $\frac{1}{d^2}$, where d = distance from the lamp.
- Volume of gas collected is equal to $\pi r^2 h$, where r = radius of capillary tube bore and h = length of bubble in capillary tube.
- Rate of photosynthesis is calculated using the volume of oxygen produced in a given time.

ecord your results here.

nalysis of results

alculate $\frac{1}{d^2}$, where d = distance from the lamp. Plot this against rate of oxygen production n an appropriate graph.

Record your processed data here (or print out the spreadsheet and stick it in here).

lot your graph here.

Conclusion (How does light intensity affect the rate of photosynthesis?)

Questions

1 Describe a suitable control for this experiment that would demonstrate that light is the factor affecting the production of oxygen gas.

2 Heat from the lamp could affect the rate of photosynthesis. How could the design of the experiment be change to reduce this?

3 Apart from light intensity, which factors can affect the rate of photosynthesis?

4 What additional measurements would ensure your results are reliable?

PAG 11 | 12

CPAC links		Evidence	Done
2a	Correctly uses appropriate instrumentation, apparatus and materials (including ICT) to carry out investigative activities, experimental techniques and procedures with minimal assistance or prompting.	Planning and practical procedure	
2d	Selects appropriate equipment and measurement strategies in order to ensure suitably accurate results.	Planning	
3a	Identifies hazards and assesses risks associated with these hazards, making safety adjustments as necessary, when carrying out experimental techniques and procedures in the lab or field.	Risk assessment	
4b	Obtains accurate, precise and sufficient data for experimental and investigative procedures and records this methodically using appropriate units and conventions.	Planning and results table	
5a	Uses appropriate software and/or tools to process data, carry out research and report findings.	Spreadsheet, research done	
5b	Sources of information are cited, demonstrating that research has taken place, supporting planning and conclusions.	Report with citations	

Objectives

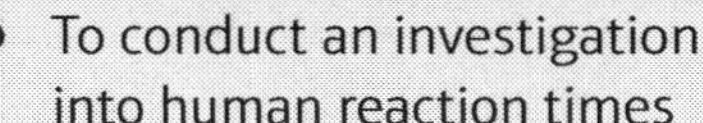

- To conduct an investigation into human reaction times
- To research the main factors that determine and limit reaction times
- To research the basic biology behind multiple sclerosis

Equipment

- metre ruler
- stop clock

Safety

- Conduct your own risk assessment with guidance from your teacher.

Procedure

Plan an investigation of your own into human reaction times. You might consider investigating factors such as the effect of caffeine, the time of day, the amount of practice someone has had, the gender of the subject or an idea of your own.

The following web resources are good starting points, but do not copy ideas or text directly from these investigations. Use your own words to explain and justify your approach. Include references and a bibliography. Ask your teacher for guidance on the correct way to do this.

- Visit www.nuffieldfoundation.org and search for the protocol 'Measuring reaction time of a human nerve-controlled reaction'.
- Visit https://faculty.washington.edu and search for 'reaction test' to find an online simulation that tests your reaction time.

You will need to consider which variables to control and how to make the method repeatable and reliable. If appropriate, conduct a risk assessment before starting.

Write your risk assessment here, then get it checked.

Write your plan here.

Record your results here.

Analysis of results

- Calculate means and standard deviations where data allows.
- Consider using a statistical test as guided by your teacher.

ecord your processed data here (or print out the spreadsheet and stick it in here).

4 Conduct some research into the factors that determine and limit the reaction times you measure. Key aspects include speed of nerve impulse transmission, synapses, myelination, saltatory conduction and nerve paths.

5 Include all of the points above in a scientific report on your investigation. This report should outline your planning, implementation, analysis of results and evaluation. Relate your research to your results.

Learning tip

- Key concepts to investigate and include in your report are: depolarisation, speed of nerve impulse transmission, synapses, myelination, nodes of Ranvier, myelin sheath and saltatory conduction.

Write your notes on your research for preparing your investigation write-up here.

Conduct further research into multiple sclerosis. Write a report on this disease which uses and relates to the knowledge you have gained from your research on reaction times. Key aspects include the myelin sheath, saltatory conduction and autoimmune reaction.

rite your notes and citations for preparing your report here.

Questions

1 List the main parts of the nervous system that an impulse will go through when a subject responds in the reaction time test.

....

....

....

....

2 Draw a typical reflex arc, such as that of the knee jerk reflex or blink reflex.

3 How does the reflex arc you described in question 2 differ from the path you gave in your answer to question 1?

....

....

....

....

AG **3**

PAC links		Evidence	Done
a	Correctly follows instructions to carry out the experimental techniques or procedures.	Practical procedure	
b	Carries out techniques or procedures methodically, in sequence and in combination, identifying practical issues and making adjustments when necessary.	Practical procedure	
a	Makes accurate observations relevant to the experimental or investigative procedure.	Results table and line profile	

Objective 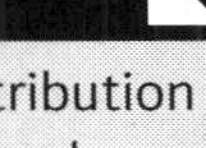

- To investigate the distribution of plant species in a sand dune

Equipment

- 50 m or 100 m measuring tape
- identification key, samples or sheet of illustrations for identification
- two ranging poles or metre rulers
- 1 m length of string
- spirit level
- recording sheet, pencil and clipboard
- clear plastic bag to protect the recording sheet from rain
- small specimen tubes or plastic bags with labels (if collecting samples)

Safety 

- Tell your teacher if you or anyone in your group is allergic to handling specific plant species.
- Have a supply of water, adequate sun or bad weather protection, appropriate clothing and sturdy footwear.

iagram

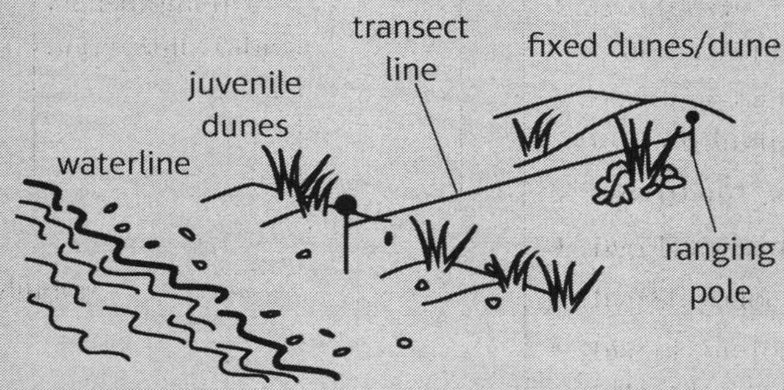

rocedure

Lay the measuring tape across the sand dunes from the edge of the first juvenile dune to the back of the shore. Secure each end firmly and keep the tape as straight as possible. This is your line transect. (If the distance is too long the tape may need to be moved after an area has been worked on.)

Use ranging poles or metre rulers and string with a spirit level to work out the profile of the dunes. Place the first pole at the start and the second pole a metre away. Run the string from the top of the first pole horizontally to the second pole. Use the spirit level to ensure the string is completely level. Record the position of the string on the second pole. Move the poles to the next position. Continue until you have moved across the whole area of study.

Starting at the juvenile dune, begin identifying and recording any species that touch the line for a distance of 5 m along the line. Make a note of any abiotic features particular to that part of the dune.

Move forwards 5 m and begin sampling again. In this way, work along the line, moving it when necessary.

Record all data in a suitable table. When sampling is complete, draw a line profile of the area with a key. Use this to show the plant distribution.

earning tips

A change in the type of species found in a habitat over time is called succession. This change is a result of changing environmental conditions.

Shifting sand dunes allow succession to be observed at a given time. This is not normally possible in other habitats.

Record your data here.

raw your profile here (leave space for a key).

Questions

1 Describe the dominant species in the juvenile dune and suggest which features allow this particular species to grow successfully in this habitat.

....

....

....

....

....

2 You will notice a change in species as you move along the line. Suggest any biotic and abiotic factors that may have influenced the change in species as you move along the line.

....

....

....

....

....

3 As you move along the line, what happens to the first dominant species that you recorded in the juvenile dune? What types of species are recorded on the mature dunes?

....

....

....

....

....

....

....

....

....

4 Suggest how you could modify this investigation to allow you to draw a kite diagram of the species recorded.

....

....

....

....

....

AG 6

:PAC links		Evidence	Done
:a	Correctly follows instructions to carry out the experimental techniques or procedures.	Practical procedure	
:a	Correctly uses appropriate instrumentation, apparatus and materials (including ICT) to carry out investigative activities, experimental techniques and procedures with minimal assistance or prompting.	Practical procedure	
3b	Uses appropriate safety equipment and approaches to minimise risks with minimal prompting.	Practical procedure	
'a	Makes accurate observations relevant to the experimental or investigative procedure.	Diagrams	

Objective

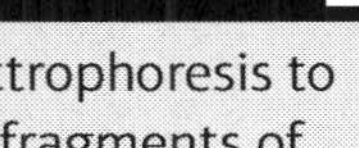

- To use gel electrophoresis to separate DNA fragments of different sizes

Equipment

- electrophoresis tanks and power supply
- 20 cm^3 agarose gel (the exact amount needed will depend on the size of gel tank used)
- 10 cm^3 dilute buffer solution
- 10 cm^3 syringe
- micropipette with micropipette tips
- two 9 V batteries
- two DNA samples or four coloured dyes
- piece of black card or paper
- protective gloves

Safety

- You should be given a full risk assessment for gel electrophoresis. Follow it carefully.

iagram

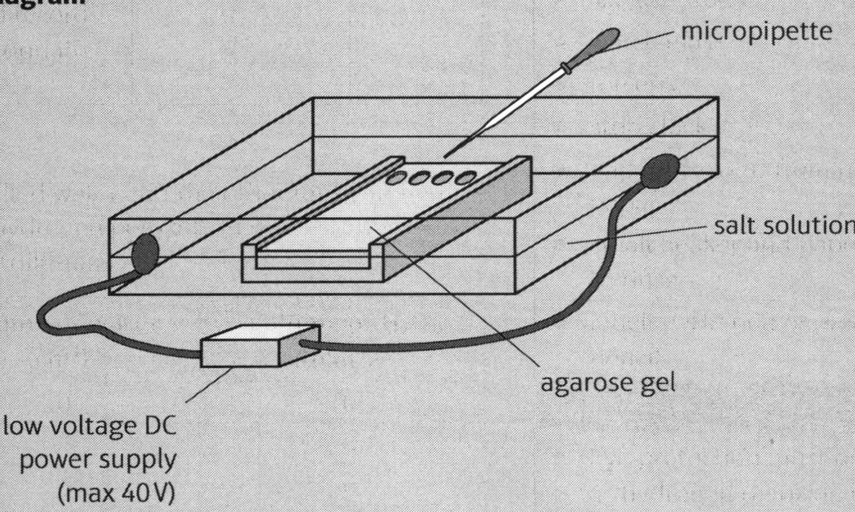

rocedure

ou will use a specially supplied kit to investigate DNA separation. Restriction nzymes are used to cut DNA samples and a technique called gel electrophoresis used to separate DNA.

Put on the gloves. Carefully remove the comb from the gel to leave four wells.

Fit the two pieces of electrode materials to either end of the tank so that the ends dip into the channels at the end.

Use the 10 cm^3 syringe to add 10 cm^3 buffer solution to the tank so that the ends of the electrode material are wet.

Use the micropipette to add 2 ml of DNA sample 1 into the second well. It will sink to the bottom of the well as it is denser than the buffer.

Use a clean micropipette tip to add 2 ml of DNA sample 2 into the fourth well.

Connect the electrical leads to the correct terminals of the power pack and switch the power pack on.

7 Watch until the samples move across the gel towards the other end. Do not allow to overrun.

8 Switch off the power immediately and observe the spread of the samples.

9 Draw diagrams to show how the fragments have been separated by this process for both samples.

Learning tips

- Electrophoresis is a separation technique used to separate DNA fragments after hydrolysis with a restriction enzyme.
- Restriction enzymes cut DNA into many fragments of different sizes. The larger and heavier the fragment, the more slowly it moves through the gel when an electric current is passed through it. This is similar to chromatography, as the smallest fragments move the furthest and the largest fragments move the least in a fixed period of time.

Record your observations here.

Analysis of results

Depending on the kit used and the aim of the activity, compare the separated DNA fragments. These can be used to identify an unknown in your samples (genetic fingerprinting).

ecord your analysis here.

uestions

Electrophoresis is a separation technique that has some similarities with the separation of particles by chromatography. Complete the following table comparing electrophoresis and chromatography.

	Electrophoresis	**Chromatography**
Components separated by:		
Medium is:		
Used to separate:		

Explain how this process can be used in forensic science to aid identification.

....

....

....

....

....

....

....

....

3 The figure below shows the results of gel electrophoresis carried out on DNA from a blood stain from a crime scene and DNA from four possible suspects. Use this data to suggest the most likely suspect in the criminal cas

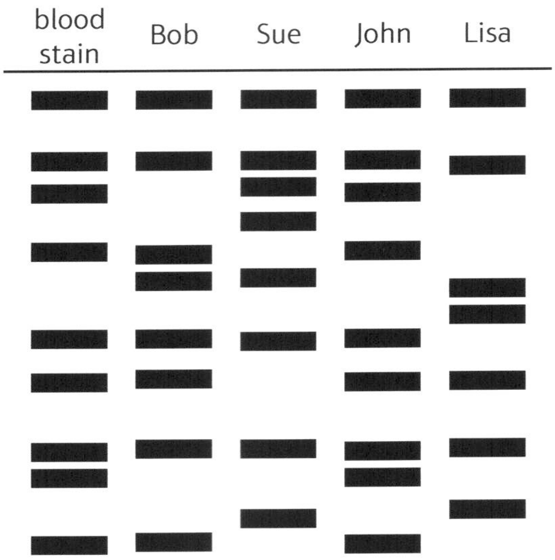

blood stain | Bob | Sue | John | Lisa

....

....

....

....

4 What are the limitations of this method of identification?

....

....

....

....

....

....

....

5 Identify the control measures that must be in place in order to be confident of any conclusions drawn.

....

....

....

....

....

....

....

PAG 11

CPAC links		Evidence	Done
1a	Correctly follows instructions to carry out the experimental techniques or procedures.	Practical procedure	
2a	Correctly uses appropriate instrumentation, apparatus and materials (including ICT) to carry out investigative activities, experimental techniques and procedures with minimal assistance or prompting.	Practical procedure	
2b	Carries out techniques or procedures methodically, in sequence and in combination, identifying practical issues and making adjustments when necessary.	Practical procedure and answers to questions	
4b	Obtains accurate, precise and sufficient data for experimental and investigative procedures and records this methodically using appropriate units and conventions.	Practical procedure	

Objectives

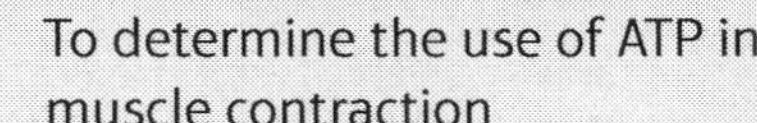

- To determine the use of ATP in muscle contraction
- To investigate muscle contraction

Equipment

- glass slide
- small piece of muscle fibre
- scalpel and two seekers
- ruler
- 0.5 cm^3 distilled/deionised water
- 0.5 cm^3 glucose solution
- 0.5 cm^3 ATP solution
- three dropping pipettes
- filter paper
- paper towels

Safety

- Wash your hands with soap and water at the end of the practical.

iagram

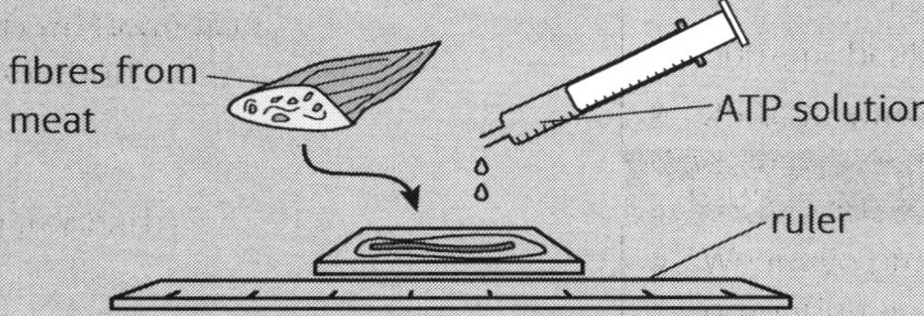

rocedure

Wipe dry a clean glass slide using a paper towel.

From a very fine strand of muscle fibre no less than 30 mm long, tease out several fibres so the muscle is about 3 mm wide.

Place the fibres onto the glass slide, keeping them as straight as possible, and measure the length in millimetres.

Add 2–3 drops of distilled water to the fibres and leave for 1 minute before measuring the length again in millimetres.

Use a piece of filter paper to soak up the distilled water. Take care not to press on the muscle fibre, or the length may be affected.

Add 2–3 drops of glucose solution to the muscle fibres. Leave for 1 minute before re-measuring the fibres.

Carefully blot off the glucose using filter paper, again taking care not to press on the fibres.

Add 2–3 drops of ATP solution to the muscle and leave for 1 minute before measuring the fibres again.

Record your results in a suitable table.

0 Calculate the percentage change in length of the fibres after each stage.

Learning tips

- ATP or adenosine triphosphate is a vital temporary energy store.
- ATP yields 31 kJ of energy per molecule.
- Each molecule of glucose releases enough energy for 30 ATP molecules to be formed during aerobic respiration.

Record your results and calculations here.

Analysis of results

1 How variable were the class results? Suggest reasons for any variation.

....

....

....

....

....

....

....

2 Suggest a way that the variability could be measured.

....

....

....

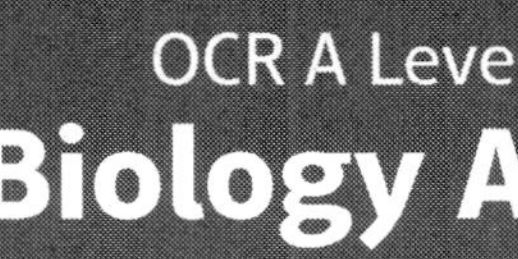

uestions

Suggest why a narrow, long strip of muscle fibre was required for this experiment.

....

....

Describe and explain the effect of each solution on the muscle fibres and explain the purpose of adding distilled water to the fibres first.

....

....

....

....

....

....

....

....

Describe the three main limitations of this procedure and suggest an improvement for each one.

....

....

....

....

....

....

....

....

....

How reliable is the data you have collected from this experiment? What could you do to make it more reliable?

....

....

....

Use your biological knowledge to describe how ATP is used in muscle contraction.

....

....

....

....

Practical 1
Analysis of results

Results will depend on the 'unknown' solution, which may contain one or two of the known amino acids. The amino acids in the unknown solution can be identified by comparing their spots with the spots produced by the known amino acids. You can compare the position, colour and R_f values of the spots in the mixture with the known amino acids.

Answers to questions

1 The R_f values calculated are for the same solvent and an identical chromatography procedure. However, there may be slight variations in the class results, due to the uncertainty involved in measuring the distance to the centre of each spot. Visual estimation of the position of the centre of the spot is difficult when the spot is elongated.

2 The solvent rises up the paper by capillary action, carrying the amino acids that are dissolved in it. The more soluble an amino acid is in the solvent, the further up the paper it will move.

3 Amino acids differ in the structure of their R group. Amino acids with different R groups have different solubility.

4 The R_f value of a particular substance should always be the same, provided the chromatogram is treated in the same manner in each case, using the same solvent. In reality, R_f values will differ slightly as a result of factors such as the type of paper used, the concentration of the solvent, the purity of the amino acid samples and the temperature.

Practical 2
Answers to questions

1 The solution in each tube is one tenth of the concentration of the preceding solution (divide by 10 each time).
Compared to the original (100%), the fractions (and %) in each tube are as follows.
Tube 2: $\frac{1}{10}$ (10%)
Tube 3: $\frac{1}{100}$ (1%)
Tube 4: $\frac{1}{1000}$ (0.1%)
Tube 5: $\frac{1}{10000}$ (0.01%)
Tube 6: $\frac{1}{100000}$ (0.001%)

2 Contamination will change the dilution by making the solution stronger or weaker than intended.

3 Serial dilutions are important when you need to know the exact dilution to calculate data, such as viable bacterial counts or yeast counts. Serial dilutions may also be used for calculating the water potential of a solution using plant tissue.

Practical 3
Analysis of results

A suitable table will record the final colour for each glucose concentration and also for the control.

You could also take photographs to support the colours recorded.

The 'unknown' glucose solution should be 1%.

Answers to questions

1 When heated strongly, glucose and Benedict's solution form a brick-red precipitate. There is no colour change when distilled water is heated with Benedict's solution (the control) so the solution will remain blue.

2 The test was repeated using distilled water so that the negative result could be compared with the positive results. This is a control test.

3 Donation of the electrons from glucose reduces the blue copper(II) ion in copper sulfate to red copper(I) oxide. Ask your teacher about the necessary chemistry or research it for yourself.

4 No. This is a qualitative test to show the presence or absence of a particular substance. It cannot measure concentration (although you can estimate an approximate range of concentrations by comparing the colours of the solutions). In addition, this reaction is not specific to glucose – other reducing sugars may cause the colour change seen in the unknown sample.

5 Use a colorimeter to measure absorbance and compare this to the absorbance of colour changes from known concentrations.

Practical 4
Analysis of results

Plot the graph (your calibration curve) showing absorbance on th y-axis against mass of glucose on the x-axis.

Include a line (or curve) of best fit.

Answers to questions

1 The glucose content of the fruit juice will depend on the juice available.

2 Not all the reducing sugar present in the juice will be glucose. Most fruit juices contain a high concentration of fructose, whi is also a reducing sugar.

3 You must test each concentration in exactly the same way so that you can be confident of the accuracy of the colorimeter readings.

4 There will be more residue left by the higher concentrations o glucose. The 0% solution will leave no residue. The mass of th residue could be taken as a semi-quantitative measure of the amount of glucose present in an unknown concentration.

5 Difficulties may depend on the type of fruit juice used. For example, it may be difficult to determine the exact colour wit juices that have a thick consistency. In this case, you may nee to dilute the juice before carrying out the experiment. You ma need to change the colorimeter filter according to the colour fruit juice used.

Practical 5
Analysis of results

A suitable table will have concentration of H_2O_2 (%) as the independent variable and time for the disc to reach the surface a the dependent variable. The three repeats and the mean value o the time taken should all be shown.

The most suitable presentation of the data is a line graph, becau the independent variable – time – is continuous.

If a trend can be identified, a line (or curve) of best fit should be drawn.

Answers to questions

1 The results should show an increase in the rate of reaction (i.e the discs rise to the surface more quickly) as the substrate concentration increases, up to V_{max} of the enzyme.

2 The reaction between the catalase and the hydrogen peroxide produces oxygen gas. The release of this oxygen lifts the discs from the bottom of the tubes to the top of the solution.

3 You should be able to use your biological knowledge on enzy to discuss:
- enzyme action
- formation of enzyme–substrate complexes
- frequency of collisions
- V_{max} of the enzymes
- activation energy.

4 Limitations include the following.
- Using the same substrate for the replicates as the concentration will have changed with each trial.
- 100% celery extract is not the same as 100% catalase. This could lead to inaccurate results as the actual catalase concentration may vary between celery sources.
- Soaking all three discs together means some will be in the extract for longer and may take up more enzyme.

5 It is not possible to overcome all the limitations in this investigation. However, modifications could include:
- using separate samples of (the same) celery extract for soa each disc
- leaving each disc to soak for exactly the same length of tim

Practical 6
Analysis of results

A suitable table will have pH as the independent variable and volume of gas produced in 15 minutes as the dependent variabl

If repeat measurements have been made (e.g. by pooling class data), the repeats and the mean value of the time taken should be shown.

The reaction rate is the rate of oxygen production in $cm^3/15$ min

ıe most suitable presentation of the data is a line graph.

a trend can be identified a line (or curve) of best fit should be drawn.

ıe reaction will be fastest at a particular pH – the optimum for the ızyme – and slower at pH values above and below this.

ıe optimum pH for catalase is approximately 7. (The result can ıly be approximate because only one pH between pH 6 and pH 8 ıs tried.) The exact pH depends on the source organism – some ngal/bacterial catalases have a pH as low as 4, while other talases have a pH above 9.

ıswers to questions

The gas produced is oxygen. The equation for this reaction is:

$$2H_2O_2 \xrightarrow{\text{catalase}} O_2 + 2H_2O$$

Answer should include:

- changes in pH affect the ionic bonds in the enzyme molecule, in particular at the active site
- these changes lead to a reduction in collisions and a reduction in the number of enzyme–substrate complexes formed.

Different enzymes are affected differently by pH changes because the number of ionic bonds present at the active site differs between enzymes. Each enzyme has its own optimum pH.

You should be able to identify any anomalous results and relate them to a specific part of the procedure. For example, an error in measuring 10 cm^3 of hydrogen peroxide could lead to inconsistencies in the volume of oxygen produced. Anomalously low volumes could indicate oxygen has escaped. Collating and comparing class results could help to identify anomalies in individual sets of data.

The main limitations are:

- the escape of gas when attaching the rubber bung and connecting the delivery tube – this will result in a lower volume of gas being collected
- variations in the time delay when adding the enzyme to each tube – this will also lead to variations in the volume of gas collected.

Modifications could include the following.

- Reducing the numbers of connectors, for example, by using a side-arm test tube with a long-angled delivery tube that can be connected directly to the inverted measuring cylinder. This will reduce gas leakage.
- Using a syringe with a needle to add the catalase directly into the boiling tube via the rubber bung. This will also reduce gas leaks. (There are safety implications here, so for further work such as an individual project/investigation, a technician could produce rubber bungs with needles already inserted.)

ractical 7
nalysis of results

ıe reaction rate for each temperature is calculated from the time ken to reach the point at which the blue-black colour no longer ɔpears.

line graph of reaction rate against temperature should have rate ı the *y*-axis and temperature on the *x*-axis.

a trend can be identified, a line (or curve) of best fit should be drawn.

ıe rate increases with temperature to a peak, then declines. There an optimum temperature at which the enzyme produces the ghest reaction rate.

nswers to questions

The starch was made up with a buffer solution to control any variation in pH by maintaining a constant pH.

The boiling tubes and test tubes were left in the water baths for 5 minutes before the enzyme and starch were mixed so that the temperature could equilibrate, i.e. to ensure each solution was at the correct temperature before it was mixed.

pH; volume and concentration of enzyme; volume and concentration of starch; number of drops of iodine solution.

You should explain that the amylase breaks down the starch, so the blue colour that starch gives with iodine decreases in intensity. Once all the starch has been broken down, there will be no blue colour at all; this is the end point.

You should include your biological knowledge of enzymes and the effect of increasing temperature on enzyme action as well as on the starch and iodine reaction. You should also refer to hydrolysing, glycosidic bonds, rate of reaction, collisions, active sites and enzyme–substrate complexes.

5 The spotting tile method with an indicator solution is not very accurate, because the measurement of the end point of the reaction is subjective – people may judge the end point differently. The method could be improved by using a comparison tube containing buffered starch solution, amylase and iodine solution that have been left until they have reacted fully; all tiles could be compared with this standard throughout the experiment. Alternatively, a colorimeter or light sensor could be used to take a quantitative reading, to avoid subjective visual methods. (If using a colorimeter or light sensor, measure absorbance at 15 s intervals until there is little change in absorbance.)

Taking samples every minute does not allow accurate determination of when the end point is reached. The time interval could be reduced to 30 s.

Practical 8
Analysis of results

A suitable table will have temperature as the independent variable and absorbance as the dependent variable. Use the actual temperature in each water bath. Any repeats and the mean value of the absorbance should all be shown.

If there are any anomalies (results that show a substantial deviation from the general pattern of results), the tests that produced these results should be repeated (where possible) and a new mean should be calculated.

A line graph of absorbance against temperature should have absorbance on the *y*-axis and temperature on the *x*-axis.

If a trend can be identified, a line (or curve) of best fit should be drawn.

Answers to questions

1 The class may have used beetroot cylinders of different lengths, or the actual temperatures in the water baths may have varied. Each student will have been using a different beetroot. Fingerprints on the colorimeter tubes could affect the transmission of light.

2 The temperature must be equilibrated to ensure the tubes contain water at the correct temperature before the experiment is started. This means you can be confident that you are assessing the effects of the correct temperature.

3 The cylinders are washed and dried to remove excess surface pigment from the cut cells at the edges of the cylinders. Any excess pigment would distort the absorbance readings, giving inaccurate results.

4 The variables controlled during the experiment are:

- the volume of water in each tube
- the size and surface area of the beetroot cylinders
- the equilibration time
- the soaking time for the cylinders
- the volume of coloured liquid in the cuvettes
- the colorimeter filter/wavelength used
- the age, variety and storage time of the beetroot (the same beetroot or beetroots from the same batch may have been used).

5 The per cent absorption increases as the temperature rises. You should use values from your own graph, for example: from 30 °C to 60 °C there is a steady increase in absorption; at around 60 °C, the absorption increases sharply.

At higher temperatures, such as 80 °C, there may be a drop in absorption before there is a further increase.

6 Molecules are continuously moving because of their kinetic energy. Movement of the phospholipids in the bilayer and movement of the pigment molecules cause pigment to leak out. The higher the temperature, the faster the movement of the molecules, and the more pigment leaves through the membrane.

7 There will be a sudden increase in per cent absorption around 60 °C; this is when lipids begin to melt and proteins begin to unravel. At very high temperatures, the protein molecules in the membrane will become completely denatured and the membrane will develop holes or gaps through which the pigment can flood out. The decrease in absorption sometimes seen at 63 °C may be because melting lipids fill the gaps before the membrane finally breaks down completely. This is a good point for discussing anomalies: although this decrease in absorption appears to be anomalous, it can be explained.

Practical 9
Analysis of results

Tables used to display results should have the independent variable (concentration/mol dm^{-3}) in the first column and the number of cells showing plasmolysis in the columns to the right. The percentage of cells showing plasmolysis should be in the far right column for each concentration.

The most suitable presentation of the data is a line graph, with concentration/mol dm^{-3} on the *x*-axis and the percentage of cells showing plasmolysis on the *y*-axis.

If a trend can be identified, a line (or curve) of best fit should be drawn.

Calculation of osmotic potential will depend on your results. You will need to estimate between points on the table.

Drawings

Your drawings should:
- use clear, unbroken lines with no shading
- label and identify features such as the cell wall
- include a title stating what the specimen is
- include the magnification at which you made your observations. For example, with an eyepiece lens magnification of ×10 and an objective of ×10, the total magnification will be ×100. Remember, this is not the same as the magnification of the drawing.

Answers to questions

1 **a** The solution closest to 50% plasmolysis will vary according to the tissue that is used, but there should be a clear point at which it occurs.

b At the point of 50% plasmolysis, the concentration of the external solution is very similar to the concentration of the cell contents.

2 When 50% of the cells show plasmolysis, net osmosis of water out of the cells is just beginning and the pressure potential has just reached zero. Therefore, the water potential is equal to the solute potential.

3 There is no specific right answer because it depends on the type of onion used, the age of the onion, and other factors, such as temperature. However, typical results would show 50% plasmolysis between 0.1 mol dm^{-3} and 0.3 mol dm^{-3} glucose. Therefore, the water potential would be between 300 kPa and 800 kPa.

4 The cells begin to take in water, reversing the effects of plasmolysis; they begin to show full turgor.

5 The number of cells counted in each sample (25 cells) is suitable and allows estimation of the osmotic potential from a graph. However, in the final calculations, each cell accounts for 4% of the sample; this reduces the accuracy of the calculations, so a larger sample size would be better.

Interpretation of cells as plasmolysed or not is somewhat subjective and there is no clear cut-off. This may reduce accuracy.

Practical 10
Risk assessment

A hazard is a potential source of harm. Possible hazards (things that could cause an injury) include use of a chemical that is an irritant, use of a sharp scalpel and touching broken glass.

Your risk assessment should list each hazard and say:
- how badly a person could be harmed by that hazard
- the likelihood of the hazard (how likely it is to happen)
- the controls you will put in place to prevent the hazard or minimise the risk involved (such as wearing eye protection, cutting away from the body, placing filter paper over the coverslip before pressing down on it)
- any further action that may be needed if the hazard happens (for example, if skin contact with a chemical occurs, washing the area thoroughly with water for 10 minutes; mopping up spillage immediately).

It is often best to present a risk assessment in the form of a table.

Drawing

Your drawings should:
- use clear, unbroken lines with no shading
- label and identify features such as the chromosomes
- show the relative sizes and positions of the chromosomes for each cell
- include annotations to describe what is happening
- include a title stating what the specimen is
- include the magnification at which you made your observations (for example, with an eyepiece lens magnification of ×10 and an objective of ×10, the total magnification will be ×100; remember this is not the same as the magnification of the drawing)
- include a scale bar, drawn with a ruler (this shows how much bigger your drawing is than the size of the image)
- clearly record measurements of the width of the cells and the length of the chromosomes.

Analysis of results

The magnification will depend on the size of the drawing and the objective used. You should divide the image size (length of scale bar measured with a ruler, converted to μm) by the actual size (the length that the scale bar represents in μm).

Answers to questions

1 Each stage of mitosis takes a different time to complete. It is possible to assess how long each stage takes relative to the others by comparing the number (percentage) of cells at each stage in a field of view. The lower the percentage of cells in a phase, the less time the cells spend in that stage. The percentage of cells in anaphase or telophase should be the lowest.

2 The root tip is heated with acid to break up the tissues into individual cells.

3 If you twist the microscope slide when pressing down, you could crack the coverslip or mix the cells so that it is difficult to identify the growing tip.

4 Pressing the preparation will separate the dividing cells into individual cells in a single layer. This makes it easier to see the different stages.

5 Take a large number of measurements/repeats for each stage and calculate mean values.

The volume of the cells would be a better descriptor of size than the linear dimensions.

Control variables, e.g. distance from root tip/age of root/use the same root.

Practical 11
Variables

Key factors to be controlled could include:
- temperature
- shape of the block
- size of the block
- immersion method
- volume of acid used
- depth of acid used
- type of agar used.

Analysis of results

The table used to display results should have the independent variable (side length of the agar cube/mm) in the first column and the time for the pink colour to disappear on the right.

Cube side length/mm	Surface area/mm^2	Volume/ mm^3	*SA* : *V*	Time taken/s

y to collect repeat data from other groups and calculate a mean. en add error bars to your graph to show the range of results from e repeats.

ot the graph showing time on the *y*-axis against *SA* : *V* on the axis.

a trend can be identified, a line (or curve) of best fit should be awn.

e *SA* : *V* ratio decreases as the side length of the agar block creases. This relationship is not linear.

e graph should show that an increase in the *SA* : *V* ratio decreases e time taken for the pink colour to disappear. The trend line ould be steeper at smaller *SA* : *V* ratios, becoming less steep as e *SA* : *V* ratio increases.

nswers to questions

The prediction should link changes in the diffusion rate with changes in the surface area : volume ratio. Increasing the *SA* : *V* ratio will increase the rate of diffusion; decreasing the *SA* : *V* ratio will decrease the rate of diffusion.

The rate of diffusion is proportional to the square of the diffusion distance. If the shortest distance to the centre of the cube is doubled, it should take four times as long for the HCl to diffuse to the centre. For example, if the distance to the centre of the cube increases from 4 mm to 8 mm (a factor of 2), the time taken for the colour to disappear should take 4 times as long (a factor of 2^2).

You can improve the reliability of your results by repeating the task at least twice. You can also pool results within the class and calculate a mean result.

A decrease in the surface area : volume ratio will cause a reduction in the rate of diffusion. This is important in living organisms because larger animals have a smaller surface area : volume ratio, so they cannot obtain sufficient nutrients and oxygen by diffusion alone. This also explains features such as the alveoli in the lungs and the villi in the intestines; these structures increase the surface area for diffusion of oxygen and nutrients.

Limitations include:
- difficulty in cutting and measuring the agar cubes accurately
- difficulty in maintaining a constant shape of agar cube
- difficulty in determining the exact end point when judging the colour change by eye
- random uncertainties in timing how long the colour takes to disappear; these will have a particularly large effect with the smallest block, which will change colour within a few seconds
- the agar blocks may float, which will affect the diffusion rate as they will not be completely submerged.

ractical 12
nswers to questions

The part of the trace that rises and drops the least represents the tidal volume, which is the volume of air taken in and exhaled at rest. The tidal volume is usually approximately 0.5 dm^3.

The vital capacity is the maximum inhaled and exhaled breath. It is shown by the part of the trace that rises and drops the most.

Readings should be around 4 dm^3.

It is impossible to measure the total lung capacity using a spirometer, because some air is retained within the lungs to prevent them collapsing. This is the residual volume. It is possible to calculate the dead space of the airways (from which there is no gaseous exchange) and the residual volume by multiplying your body mass (in kg) by 10 cm^3. Add this figure to the vital capacity to find the total lung capacity.

The peaks and troughs on the trace get lower because the oxygen within the chamber is consumed, so the volume of gas in the chamber decreases. You can find the total volume of oxygen consumed over the duration of the trace by measuring the difference between the top of the peaks at the start and the top of the peaks at the end. The carbon dioxide produced is absorbed and does not enter the chamber.

This value is dependent on you and on your activity level.

Practical 13
Drawing your dissection
- Draw what you see – do not copy from a textbook or another source.
- Use clear unbroken lines with no shading.
- Include a title stating what the specimen is.
- Add a scale bar immediately below the drawing.
- Label your diagrams clearly.
- Add annotations and measurements to each chamber.

Answers to questions

1 Observations:
- The two atria will have collapsed onto the top of the heart because they are no longer filled with blood.
- The walls of these two chambers can be stretched easily to show their relative thinness and also their inner dimensions.
- All four chambers have the same inner volume.

2 Explanations:
- The left ventricle has a very thick muscular wall to pump blood under high pressure around the whole body. It needs to contract with greater force to overcome the resistance of the systemic circulation.
- The right ventricle does not need such a thick muscular wall because the blood from this side of the heart is only pumped to the lungs. Blood entering the lungs must be at a lower pressure or the lungs will be damaged.

3 The heart strings attach the bicuspid and tricuspid valves to the ventricle walls and prevent the valves inverting. This helps to prevent any backflow of blood, so the blood can flow in one direction only.

4 Blood flows through the heart in one direction only because the heart valves are all one-way valves. These valves maintain this one-directional flow.
- A single red blood cell starting at the lungs will flow through the pulmonary vein into the left atrium of the heart. It will then pass into the left ventricle and leave the heart via the aorta. From there, it will travel to the capillaries in the body tissues.
- From the tissues, the red blood cell will travel to the vena cava until it enters the right atrium of the heart. It will then pass into the right ventricle and leave the heart via the pulmonary artery. From there, it will travel back to the lungs.

5 The coronary arteries supply the heart muscle itself with oxygen and nutrient-carrying blood. You should name a suitable nutrient (e.g. glucose).

Practical 14
Variables

A number of different environmental conditions could affect water uptake, and only one should be changed.
- Light: should be fairly constant within one lesson but could be different if the experiment is repeated on a different day. Can be controlled by using a lamp at a fixed distance and monitored using a light meter.
- Air movement/wind speed: no wind in the lab but random draughts are difficult to control.
- Temperature: lab temperature should be fairly constant within one lesson but could be different if the experiment is repeated on a different day.
- Humidity: should be fairly constant within one lesson but could be different if the experiment is repeated on a different day.

Using the same shoot for each condition will ensure that variables relating to the plant shoot, such as leaf area and stomatal density, remain constant

Analysis of results

A suitable table will have environmental condition (such as normal, dark, moving air, high humidity) as the independent variable and the time taken for the bubble to move a set distance as the dependent variable.

The volume and the rate of water uptake should also be shown. Units for rate are typically $mm^3\ min^{-1}$. Calculate the volume using the formula for the volume of a cylinder: $V = \pi r^2 h$. In this case, h is the distance moved by the bubble.

If repeat measurements have been made (e.g. by pooling class data), the repeats and the mean value of the time taken should also be shown in the table.

Answers to questions

1 Measurements of the rate of water uptake made using the potometer equipment are not exactly equal to the rate of water loss by transpiration. This is because water may be used up or produced by metabolic processes in plant cells. However, the volume of water involved in metabolic processes is insignificant/very small in comparison with the large volume flowing through the plant in the transpiration stream. This means it is reasonable to assume that the rate of water loss by transpiration equals the rate of water uptake. To measure water loss directly, you could measure loss in mass.

2 If the seal is not airtight, water will not be drawn up the capillary tube and there will be no movement of the air bubble.

3 Limitations that could alter the rate of transpiration include:
- the size of the shoot
- the number of leaves on the shoot
- the total surface area of the leaves.

Limitations that could slow water movement include:
- the difficulty in making a seal between the shoot and the apparatus.

4 Effects of these limitations are:
- transpiration rate will increase if a larger leaf surface area is used or if there are more leaves present and vice versa
- lack of an airtight seal will slow the movement of the air bubble and may stop transpiration altogether; this will give a lower value for the rate of water uptake.

5 The following measures can be taken to reduce limitations.
- Shoots must be the same size, with the same surface area of leaves.
- The seal between the shoot and the apparatus must be as airtight as possible (this may be achieved by fitting a flexible material, such as plumber's putty, to the neck of the potometer to hold the shoot and act as a seal).
- Repeating the experiment two more times will give a measure of reliability and will allow you to calculate a mean. You could compare your results with the results of the rest of the class.

6 To compare different shoots, you must take into account the leaf area of each shoot. To do this, determine the leaf area of each shoot and convert your results into volume of water per unit of leaf area per unit time, e.g. $mm^3\ m^{-2}\ hour^{-1}$. Divide your water uptake rate results by the leaf area from your measurements.

Practical 15

Sample results table

Quadrat	No. of individual plants			Soil moisture (%)
	Species A	Species B	Species C	
	4	4	0	2.5
	10	1	4	5.0
	9	0	8	15.3
	12	0	6	11.6
	6	5	0	3.4
	11	2	2	4.3
	4	2	0	3.2
	12	0	7	12.8
	5	0	12	15.7
	8	1	11	9.2
	7	6	4	2.1
	15	2	9	10.7
	9	3	6	8.1
	8	7	0	3.2
	6	3	1	6.3

Analysis of results

For each quadrat, plot three scatter graphs (correlation graphs) - one for each species. Your graphs should show moisture content along the *x*-axis and plant abundance on the *y*-axis.

Answers to questions

1 Answers will vary depending on the chosen site.

2 A correlation coefficient is a suitable test. Write a null hypoth and an alternative hypothesis before carrying out the statisti analysis.

3 Use the 5% significance level to determine the accuracy of yo results compared with the expected or theoretical data.

4 You should show you understand the meaning of the term 'validity'. Your conclusions may be considered valid if the data fi the theoretical/expected data well, or if the data support the nu hypothesis. If the null hypothesis is rejected and your conclusio do not support the predicted findings, then the conclusions ma not be valid. For example, results are unlikely to be valid if varia other than the independent variable have not been controlled.

5 Any valid example of an abiotic factor that may not have bee controlled, e.g. humus content, light intensity, use of fertiliser herbicide, soil pH.

6 It is important to sample randomly to get a true representati of the population and avoid investigator bias. For example, scientists might unconsciously 'choose' a sample that will support a particular hypothesis or give unfair weight to rare b highly visible species. If plants are not evenly spaced through the study area, it might be tempting to focus on areas where there are more plants. This will produce a population estimat that is greater than the true population.

7 Choosing where to stand and in which direction to throw the quadrats will introduce sample bias. Not all parts of the area have an equal chance of being sampled – the far edges (and area where the person is standing) are less likely to be sampl

Practical 16

Low power diagram

Your drawing should:
- show only the outlines of tissues
- show the structures in the correct proportions
- identify the islets of Langerhans and ducts, and show the posit of the acinar cells (write the labels outside the drawing itself)
- completely enclose each tissue with lines
- not show any individual cells
- include a title stating what the specimen is.

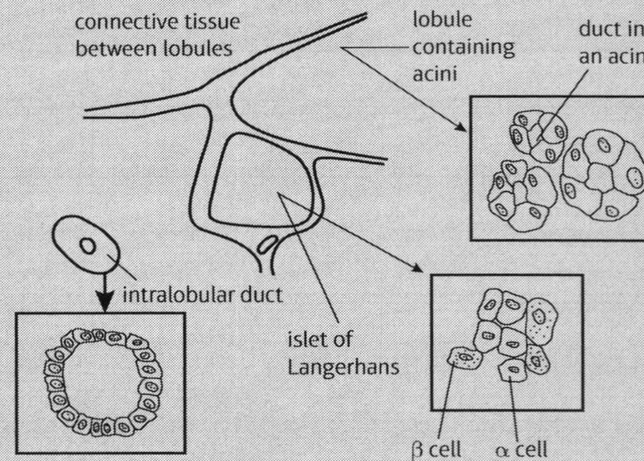

Figure A. Example drawing of a low power tissue plan. Note, the acinus is not shown

Diagrams of cells around a duct, and of islet tissue
- Include a title stating what each diagram shows.
- Only draw a few representative cells.
- If there are many similar cells, there is no need to show the cel structure for all the cells. Just show the outlines of adjacent ce to show how the cells are arranged in relation to each other.
- Individual cells drawn at high power should be about one to several centimetres in diameter.

)o not shade in nuclei – just draw the outline.
abel and identify the cells drawn.
nnotations of the identified cells should include structural etails (such as shape, size, colour and texture) and details of the ell's function.
nclude a scale bar, drawn with a ruler.
t is also useful to state the combined magnification of the yepiece plus objective lenses used.
learly record measurements of the length and breadth of the ells.
deally, measure more than one cell and calculate a mean to stimate a more reliable cell size.

swers to questions

It should be possible to identify at least two types – the α and β cells – since they are different sizes.

Either: the network of blood capillaries links to the endocrine function of the pancreas; or, larger α cells and smaller β cells each produce a different hormone.

Your answer should refer to α cells secreting glucagon and β cells secreting insulin and include the roles of these two hormones in the control of blood glucose levels. You should know the ways in which insulin reduces glucose levels and glucagon increases glucose levels in the blood.

Acinar cells are cuboidal or column-like (wedge-shaped) cells surrounding an interlobular duct. Your answer should state their function of enzyme production and secretion as well as secretion of alkaline fluid into the duct which connects to the main pancreatic ducts.

Your answers in each case will depend on the size of the drawing and the objective used. You should divide the image size (length of scale bar measured with a ruler, converted to μm) by the actual size (the length that the scale bar represents in μm).

actical 17
w power diagram
ur drawing should:
how only the outlines of tissues
how the structures in the correct proportions
how the position of the Bowman's capsule, kidney tubules and lomerulus (write the labels outside the drawing itself)
ompletely enclose each tissue with lines
ot show any individual cells
nclude a title stating what the specimen is.

agrams of cells showing the Bowman's capsule wall and omerular cells and cells of the loop of Henle and tubules of e medulla
nclude a title stating what each diagram shows.
)nly draw a few representative cells.
f there are many similar cells, there is no need to show the cell tructure for all the cells. Just show the outlines of adjacent cells o show how the cells are arranged in relation to each other.
ndividual cells drawn at high power should be about one to everal centimetres in diameter.
)o not shade in nuclei – just draw the outline.
abel and identify the cells drawn.
nnotations of the identified cells should include structural details (such as shape, size, colour and texture) and details of the ell's function.
nclude a scale bar, drawn with a ruler.
t is also useful to state the combined magnification of the yepiece plus objective lenses used.
learly record measurements of the length and breadth of the ells.

swers to questions

Your description of the Bowman's capsule cells should refer to the flattened appearance of the cells of the renal capsule, which provides a short diffusion distance. You could demonstrate biological knowledge with a reference to the podocytes, although they will not be visible at the magnifications used here. The tubules will be cut through in different planes.

2 Your answer should refer to ultrafiltration from the blood into the capsule. The thinness of the cells and the arrangement of the podocytes allow filtration under pressure. Your answer should refer to a relative molecular mass of 69 000 as the maximum size of molecules that can pass through the tissue.

3 The blood flows through the glomerulus under pressure. This is a result of arteriole pressure and of the larger afferent arteriole feeding blood into the glomerulus with a narrower efferent arteriole removing blood from the glomerulus.

4 You should refer to the proximal and distal tubules present in the cortex as well as the Bowman's capsule. Since this is a transverse section, the tubules will be cut across and will mostly have a rounded appearance. In the medulla, the loop of Henle appears as longer sections of tubule, less rounded in appearance than the cortex tubules. There are also no Bowman's capsules or glomeruli.

Practical 18
Low power diagram
Your drawing should:
- show only the outlines of tissues
- show the structures in the correct proportions
- identify the muscle fibres (write the labels outside the drawing itself)
- completely enclose each tissue with lines
- label nuclei but not show any other cellular detail
- include a title stating what the specimen is.

High power diagram of a single fibre or part of a fibre
- Include a title stating what the diagram shows.
- Only show the outlines of adjacent muscle fibres to show how these are arranged in relation to each other.
- Do not shade in nuclei – just draw the outline.
- Label and identify the features drawn.
- Annotations of features should include structural details (such as shape, size, colour and texture) and details of their function.
- Include a scale bar, drawn with a ruler.
- It is also useful to state the combined magnification of the eyepiece plus objective lenses used.
- Clearly record measurements of the width of muscle fibre and a nucleus.

Answers to questions

1 'Multinucleate' means there are many nuclei. These nuclei and other organelles share a common cytoplasm (called 'sarcoplasm' in muscle cells). There are no separate cell membranes around each nucleus or cytoplasm. (This is known as a 'multinucleate syncytium', but you are not required to know the term.)

2 The fibres are long to help span the length of a muscle and to allow contraction and relaxation lengthways in relation to the whole muscle.

3 In cardiac muscle, nuclei (and other organelles) do not share cytoplasm, so there are individual muscle cells, not multinucleate fibres. Fibres are short and have branches so contraction can spread sideways across the heart.

4 Your answer will depend on the size of the drawing and the objective used.

Practical 19
Analysis of results
The reaction involved in the biosensor:

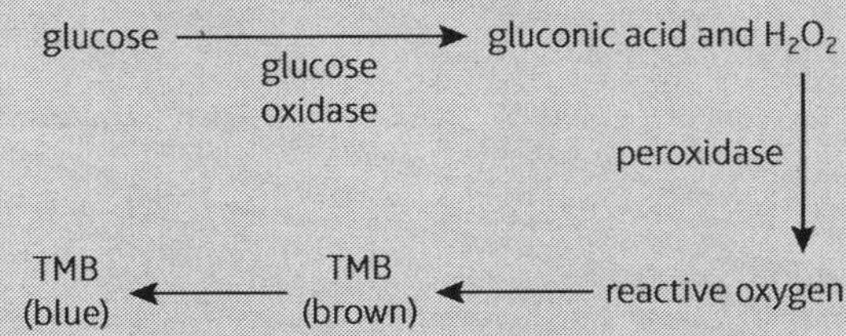

The sucrose test is the control and should give negative results. A deeper colour change should occur with higher glucose concentrations.

Sample data table

Urine sample number	Colour of biosensor
1	
2	
3	
4	
5	
Sucrose solution	

Answers to questions

1. This will be determined by the change in colour. The strength of colour will depend on the glucose concentration, and excess glucose in urine is an indicator of diabetes. Several samples may have changed colour.
2. The enzyme A would alter the colour developer B before it came into contact with the test solution.
3. This is a control, since sucrose will not react with the enzyme. A negative result shows that the reaction producing a colour change is glucose specific.

Practical 20
Analysis of results

A suitable table includes the batch number in the first column and the volume of juice collected for each batch in the columns to the right. Tables should also include any replicate data obtained from the rest of the class.

A suitable graph is a bar chart with the batch numbers on the *x*-axis and volumes of juice on the *y*-axis. A line graph is not suitable, as each batch is an independent event.

Answers to questions

1. Enzyme activity will decline over several batches, since some of the enzymes will be lost, damaged or denatured.
2. The variables to be controlled to obtain accurate and reliable data include:
   - volume of enzyme, sodium alginate, calcium chloride and apple pulp
   - pH
   - temperature
   - time
   - filtering method for each batch.
3. The main limitations and possible improvements are as follows.

Limitation	Improvement
It is difficult to keep the sizes and therefore the surface areas of alginate beads consistent.	Use a fine syringe with a dispenser to standardise the bead size.
The handling of the beads during the set-up of each batch is variable.	Handle the beads as little as possible and standardise the number of times handled and the amount of handling.
The number of enzymes within the beads damaged during each batch will vary.	This will be difficult to control practically.

4. The main advantages of using immobilised enzymes commercially include greater yield and greater efficiency. This is because continuous flow can be used rather than the batch method, meaning that there is no delay in setting up.

Practical 21
Analysis of results

A suitable table will record time as the independent variable and pH as the dependent variable.

A graph of the results should show pH against time, with time on the *x*-axis and pH on the *y*-axis.

Answers to questions

1. Subsequent samples show a slightly increasing pH, suggesting a reduction in efficiency as enzymes are lost, denatured or damaged.
2. The rate of enzyme-catalysed reactions varies with temperatu As temperature increases, particles gain more energy and mc collisions take place between enzyme and substrate particles Enzymes have an optimum temperature at which the rate of reaction is at its peak. Above that temperature, enzymes will begin to denature, changing the shape of the active site and preventing further catalysis. A water bath and thermometer could be used to maintain a suitable temperature.
3. The continuous method in this practical is preferable to the batch method used in Practical 20 because:
   - set-up time is reduced
   - handling of the immobilised enzyme is reduced
   - a more consistent product is produced.
4. The reduction in efficiency of the enzymes over time suggest that immobilised enzymes cannot be reused indefinitely with being denatured or damaged. This compromises the validity this conclusion. A statistical test could be used to demonstrat how valid the conclusion is.
5. Commercial uses of immobilised enzymes are many and changing; there is a lot of information available from general searches. Examples could include using glucose isomerase to convert glucose to fructose, or using nitrilase to convert acrylonitrile to acrylamide for use in the plastics industry.

Practical 22
Sample data analysis

Juice concentration (%)	Growth zone (mm^2)	Percentage coverage (%)
100	98	1.96
80	126	2.52
60	143	2.86
40	256	5.12
20	420	8.40
0	565	11.30

Answers to questions

1. As the concentration of the lemon juice increases, the bacteri growth decreases – there is an inverse relationship.
2. Quantitative results can be obtained as follows.
   - Use Vernier callipers to measure the diameter of each colon and calculate the area of the colony circle. However, this ma be time consuming depending on the number of colonies.
   - Place a sheet of acetate onto the base of each dish and cop the outline of bacterial growth. 1 mm^2 paper can be used to calculate the area of the colony circles.
3. A line graph is most suitable, showing dilution of lemon juice the *x*-axis and area of growth on the *y*-axis.

Practical 23
Analysis of results

A suitable table will record tube number as the independent variable and observations and/or absorbance (as a percentage), recorded, as the dependent variable.

A suitable graph is a bar chart with the tube numbers on the *x*-a and absorbance on the *y*-axis. A line graph is not appropriate.

Answers to questions

1. Oil is used to prevent oxygen entering tube B, so that yeast h to use anaerobic respiration.
2. The tubes will show distinct differences. Tube C will not chan colour during the experiment, since boiling has killed the yeast and denatured the enzymes within the cells, meaning no respiration will take place. Tube A will decolourise the blu colour substantially in 10 minutes. Tube B should begin to sh decolourisation, but will not be fully decolourised in the time

   This is explained by the differences in the type of respiration. Aerobic respiration in tube A will release a large number of hydr atoms and will therefore reduce the methylene blue rapidly. Anaerobic respiration in tube B will release only a small number hydrogen atoms, so the methylene blue will be only partly reduc

Any relevant limitation should be given a mark. The improvements must correspond to the limitations.

Suggested limitations:

- Tubes are not shaken thoroughly so the methylene blue is not evenly distributed, or tubes are shaken inconsistently so there are different distributions of methylene blue in the different tubes.
- Tubes are shaken after incubation, which will re-oxidise the contents and so give varied results.
- Colorimeter tubes are held incorrectly so that fingerprints prevent some light transmission through the tube and cause the absorbance to appear greater than it is.
- Temperature is not kept constant.

Suggested improvements:

- Give detailed steps of the exact method of shaking so that all tubes are correctly mixed.
- Give details of how the tubes can be moved without any shaking or mixing after incubation.
- Use gloves and only hold the colorimeter tubes near the top to avoid depositing grease on the tube surface.
- Use a thermostatic water bath to keep the temperature constant.

The hydrogen atoms released will reduce a hydrogen carrier such as NAD and will either be used in the electron transport chain in aerobic respiration or be used to form ethanol in anaerobic respiration in yeast.

The advantage of using colorimeter readings is that a quantitative reading can be taken to avoid subjective visual methods or recording differences.

actical 24
difying the apparatus

asuring the height of the gas bubble produced is not precise accurate, as the low resolution of the ruler scale will cause ne uncertainty in readings, as will judging the position of the niscus. The tube may also have to be taken out of the water bath ore you can measure the length of the bubble, meaning the nperature will not be constant.

table improvements include calibration of the Durham tube by rking volumes on the side of the tube with a sharp chinagraph ncil. Alternatively, the volume of gas could be worked out from height of the bubble and the cross-sectional area of the ham tube. This is not easy to measure accurately, since the tube es at the opening and has a domed end.

your graph, the independent variable (different substrates) must on the x-axis and the height of gas produced on the y-axis. The ph must be a bar chart, since a line graph is not appropriate.

swers to questions

See 'Modifying the apparatus' above. Another improvement would be to use more accurate and precise measuring apparatus such as respirometers.

Glucose and fructose usually give the highest rate of respiration. This is because these monosaccharide sugars are the usual substrates for yeast respiration. Other sugars will first need to be converted, requiring enzyme action. This will take time, and so the respiration rate will be slower.

Some sugars, such as lactose and galactose, will not be respired, since the yeast does not have the correct enzymes. These sugars are not found in the yeast's normal habitat.

ctical 25
alysis of results

uitable table will have concentration of H_2CO_3 (mol dm^{-3}) as the ependent variable and time as the dependent variable.

uitable graph is a line graph with concentration of H_2CO_3 on the kis and time (in minutes or seconds) on the y-axis (for the first ph) and 1/time (in min^{-1} or s^{-1}) on the y-axis (for the second graph).

he second graph, an increase in the carbon dioxide centration initially increases the rate of photosynthesis but the reaches a plateau at higher concentrations. This is because ally an increase in the carbon dioxide concentration increases rate at which carbon is incorporated into carbohydrate in the t-independent reaction, but at higher concentrations the rate is ted by another factor, such as temperature or light intensity.

Answers to questions

1. As the leaf cells photosynthesise, they produce oxygen gas which fills the air spaces and the discs rise.
2. We assume that the gas is oxygen, produced by photosynthesis, and that the rate of bubble formation will be directly proportional to the rate of photosynthesis. There could be a small amount of carbon dioxide in the bubbles from respiration. Some of the oxygen produced will be used internally in respiration. Nitrogen may also come out of solution in the water. The rate of respiration is likely to be constant and is unlikely to be affected by altering the concentration of sodium hydrogencarbonate. As long as the temperature remains constant, the assumption that any change in rate of gas production is due to changes in the concentration of sodium hydrogencarbonate is probably valid.
3. At low sodium hydrogencarbonate concentrations, the leaf discs will not be supplied with sufficient carbon dioxide for photosynthesis, so carbon dioxide will be a limiting factor and less gas will be produced. At higher concentrations, carbon dioxide will not be a limiting factor so more gas will be produced.
4. Temperature and light intensity are both factors affecting photosynthesis and so will affect the volume of gas produced and thus the time taken for the discs to rise.
5. You should describe the measures you took during the experiment to minimise the effect of these other factors or describe measures you would take to improve the task, for example, to quantify or control the ambient light intensity.
6. Temperature can be regulated using a greenhouse heater and carbon dioxide concentration can be increased. Regulation of light would also improve crop yield.

Practical 26
Analysis of results

You will need to calculate volume of oxygen (in cm^3) from measurements of the bubble length and the value of the radius of the capillary tube bore given to you by your teacher.

A suitable table will have distance of the lamp from the beaker (in cm) as the independent variable and volume of oxygen (cm^3) as the dependent variable. The table should then additionally show $\frac{1}{d^2}$ where d = distance from the lamp.

The graph should have the independent variable of light intensity $\left(\frac{1}{d^2}\right)$ on the x-axis and the volume of oxygen produced over 2 minutes on the y-axis. A line graph is an appropriate graph to use.

Sample data

Distance of lamp d (cm) from beaker	$\frac{1}{d^2}$	Volume of oxygen (cm^3)
10	0.0100	0.88
15	0.0044	0.81
20	0.0025	0.40
25	0.0016	0.21
30	0.0011	0.18

Answers to questions

1. The apparatus can be set up and the experiment repeated in a dark cupboard to demonstrate that light is the factor affecting the production of oxygen gas.
2. Put a transparent heat sink such as water in a flat-sided glass container between the light source and the pondweed.
3. Factors that could limit the rate of photosynthesis include temperature and carbon dioxide concentration.
4. Repeat all readings for each light intensity at least twice.

Practical 27

Possible hazards (things that could cause an injury) depend on the investigation you plan, but could include moving around the room with metre rulers, hot coffee/tea, consuming drinks in a laboratory where chemicals or biomaterials are regularly used and an adverse reaction to high levels of caffeine.

Your risk assessment should list the hazard, how badly a person could be harmed, the likelihood (how likely is it to happen), the controls you will put in place to prevent the hazard and any further action that may be needed if the hazard happens.

Your plan should include: an explanation of theory to support your practical procedure; identification of variables that must be controlled; selection of suitable equipment and how it will be used; techniques for the proposed investigation including how you will ensure the results are as accurate and reliable as possible; and the justification for each decision about the steps in the method.

Analysis of results

Your table should show the raw data collected, the mean and the standard deviation.

Standard error/95% confidence limits would be a suitable test, because you are looking for differences between mean values (of samples).

Answers to questions

1 Receptor (e.g. eye/retina); sensory nerve; spinal cord; brain (e.g. cerebellum); motor nerve; effector (e.g. muscles of hand).
2 Diagrams should be clear and show the following parts, which should be correctly connected: sensory nerve ending/receptor; sensory nerve cell axon with cell body in a ganglion; section of spinal cord to detail axons and synapses; white matter; grey matter; intermediate/bipolar nerve cell; motor nerve cell body; motor nerve endings (e.g. motor end plate in a muscle/effector).
3 A reflex arc does not include the brain but only a single intermediate nerve cell in the white matter of the spinal cord (although nerve branches do go to the brain from the arc).

Practical 28
Analysis of results

- The independent variable in this study is the distance along the line. This should be recorded in the first column of the table. Species counts and any abiotic factors can be recorded in columns to the right.
- If you do not take readings for a kite diagram, a line profile with the species recorded along it using symbols or colours is an effective graphical representation of your findings. You should include a key for the symbols or colours.

Answers to questions

1 The dominant species may be marram grass or a similar xerophyte. Xerophytes are adapted to live in environments with little or no liquid water.
2 The factors affecting the change in species will depend on the chosen site, but will certainly include moisture and humus content. Soil bacteria and the presence of other organisms will also affect the species present.
3 As the conditions change along the line:
   - The xerophytes are no longer found.
   - New species and a greater number of species appear as the environment becomes less harsh.
   - Primary succession brings some species, and later these are replaced by secondary succession species and finally the climax community.
4 To draw a kite diagram, numbers of each species need to be recorded at each point along the line. The best method is a belt transect, where quadrats are moved along the line and numbers of each species are recorded.

Practical 29
Sample data

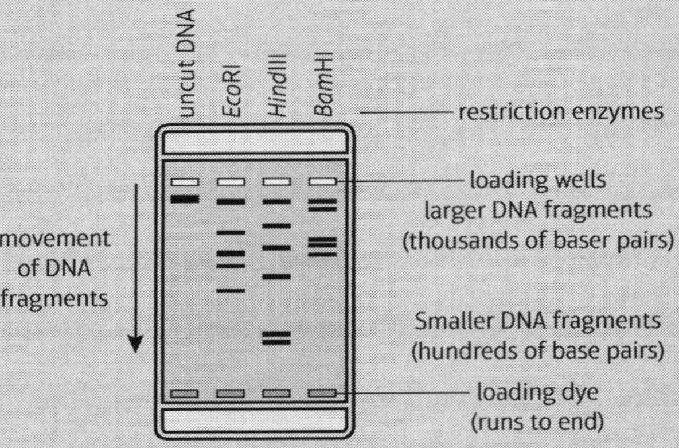

Although several possible results are shown here, note that samp are only run in lanes 2 and 4 in this practical.

Answers to questions

1

	Electrophoresis	Chromatography
Components separated by:	electric current (separates according to size/charge)	solvent (separates according to solubility)
Medium is:	gel in a gel tank	paper, thin layer pla gel or gas
Used to separate:	DNA fragments (or coloured dyes)	soluble molecules such as amino acids and sugars (or mixtures of colourec compounds, such as inks and dyes)

2 In forensic science, the DNA sample is collected and a restrict enzyme added to cut the DNA into fragments. The fragments are then separated by electrophoresis and spread across the A dye or a radioactive probe is added to make the fragments visible. The DNA has now been separated into a barcode-like spread of fragments. This can be compared with known data identify a person. This technique may be used in a criminal ca or to establish paternity.
3 John is a likely suspect as his DNA matches the blood stain found at the scene of the crime. However, this by itself canno determine that John has committed the crime. It simply place him at the scene.
4 The same restriction enzyme must be used to cut the fragme from all of the individuals involved in the identification. It cannot be used to distinguish between people with identical DNA, but since this only applies to identical twins it is not a major limitation.
5 To be confident of any conclusions drawn, the DNA must not contaminated by any other DNA. This means that in a crimina case the scene must be isolated immediately and DNA sampl must be taken from anyone known to be present, including t investigators.

Practical 30
Sample results table

Treatment	Fibre length (mm)	% change in fib length
before treatment	35	0
after distilled water	38	8.57
after glucose solution	36	2.86
after ATP solution	27	22.86

alysis of results

There will be some variation in fibre length changes due to differences in the length of the sample; this is why percentage changes are calculated. There will also be variation in the thickness of samples; ATP will diffuse more slowly through thicker strips so not all the solution may reach all the fibres and less contraction will be measured. There could be variation due to variables that are not controlled, such as breed of animal the meat came from, freshness of meat/whether it has been frozen (storage or freezing of meat may cause damage to muscle proteins, meaning less muscle contraction; temperature of storage could also vary).

Variability could be measured either as the range, or by calculating the standard deviation.

swers to questions

A narrow, long strip of muscle fibre is required so that any changes in length are clear and can easily be measured.

The distilled water is a control and any changes in length will be a result of dehydration. There may be a small amount of lengthening if the meat has been left out for a while.

Glucose alone will not affect contraction, since it is unlikely that the cells are still respiring, so they will not be able to use the glucose.

The ATP solution causes the fibres to shorten by up to 30%. The presence of ATP causes molecular changes (shortening) in muscle cells and provides energy for muscle contraction.

3 The same piece of muscle fibre is used each time, so it may stretch during blotting or dry out. The muscle fibres may not be the total length of the fibre strand, so less contraction will occur. It is also difficult to keep the fibres straight and measure them accurately.

The procedure could be improved by using a fresh piece of muscle fibre each time, cutting a few fibres from a much bigger piece of meat to ensure all the fibres are the same length, and using Vernier callipers and string to measure the length.

4 Reliability is compromised because only one set of data is collected. There should be at least three replicates.

5 You should use your knowledge of muscle contraction to describe the role of ATP in the sliding filament mechanism of muscle movement.

Practical 1

- Use appropriate units.
- Use decimal and standard form.
- Use an appropriate number of significant figures.
- Put values into an equation.

Practical 2

- Use ratios, fractions and percentages.

Practical 3

- Use appropriate units.

Practical 4

- Use an appropriate number of significant figures.
- Use appropriate units.
- Plot two variables from experimental data.
- Translate data between graphical and numerical formats.

Practical 5

- Use appropriate units.
- Use decimal and standard form.
- Use ratios, fractions and percentages.
- Use an appropriate number of significant figures.
- Calculate a mean.
- Construct and interpret frequency tables and diagrams.
- Translate data between graphical and numerical formats.
- Plot two variables from experimental data.

Practical 6

- Use appropriate units.
- Use decimal and standard form.
- Use an appropriate number of significant figures.
- Construct and interpret frequency tables and diagrams.
- Translate data between graphical and numerical formats.
- Plot two variables from experimental data.

Practical 7

- Use an appropriate number of significant figures.
- Use appropriate units.
- Plot two variables from experimental data.
- Translate data between graphical and numerical formats.

Practical 8

- Use appropriate units.
- Use decimal and standard form.
- Use an appropriate number of significant figures.
- Calculate a mean.
- Construct tables and graphs.
- Calculate standard deviation if instructed to do so by your teacher.
- Plot two variables from experimental data.

Practical 9

- Use appropriate units.
- Use decimal and standard form.
- Use ratios, fractions and percentages.

Use an appropriate number of significant figures.
Calculate a mean.
Construct and interpret frequency tables and diagrams.
Change the subject of an equation, e.g. magnification.
Put values into an equation with appropriate units, e.g. micrometres.
Translate data between graphical and numerical formats.
Plot two variables from experimental data.

actical 10

Use appropriate units.
Use decimal and standard form.
Use percentages and scales for measuring.
Use an appropriate number of significant figures.
Calculate magnification.
Change the subject of an equation, e.g. magnification.
Put values into an equation with appropriate units, e.g. micrometres.
Solve an equation, e.g. magnification.

actical 11

Use appropriate units.
Use decimal and standard form.
Use the appropriate number of significant figures.
Construct and interpret frequency tables and diagrams.
Translate data between graphical and numerical formats.
Plot two variables from experimental data.

ctical 12

Use appropriate units.
Use decimal and standard form.
Estimate results and check that the calculated values are appropriate.
Interpret data from a variety of graphs (e.g. explain spirometer or electrocardiogram traces).
Translate data between graphical and numerical formats.

actical 13

Use appropriate units.
Use decimal and standard form.
Calculate a mean.

actical 14

Use appropriate units.
Use decimal and standard form.
Use ratios, fractions and percentages.
Use the appropriate number of significant figures.
Calculate a mean.

actical 15

Construct and interpret frequency tables and diagrams.
Understand simple probability.
Understand the principles of sampling as applied to scientific data.
Use a scatter diagram to identify a correlation between two variables.
Select and use a statistical test.
Translate information between graphical, numerical and algebraic forms.
Plot two variables from experimental or other data.

Practical 16

- Use appropriate units.
- Use decimal and standard form.
- Use percentages and scales for measuring.
- Use an appropriate number of significant figures.

Practical 17

- Use appropriate units.
- Use decimal and standard form.
- Use percentages and scales for measuring.
- Use an appropriate number of significant figures.

Practical 18

- Use appropriate units.
- Use decimal and standard form.
- Use percentages and scales for measuring.
- Use an appropriate number of significant figures.

Practical 20

- Use decimal and standard form.
- Find arithmetic means.
- Construct and interpret frequency tables and diagrams, bar charts and histograms.
- Plot two variables from experimental data.

Practical 21

- Use decimal and standard form.
- Find arithmetic means.
- Construct and interpret frequency tables and diagrams.
- Plot two variables from experimental data.

Practical 22

- Use appropriate units.
- Use ratios, fractions and percentages.
- Use an appropriate number of significant figures.
- Calculate a mean.
- Construct and interpret frequency tables and diagrams.
- Translate data between graphical and numerical formats.
- Plot two variables from experimental data.

Practical 23

- Use appropriate units.
- Use decimal and standard form.
- Use an appropriate number of significant figures.
- Construct and interpret frequency tables and bar charts.
- Translate data between graphical and numerical formats.
- Plot two variables from experimental data.

Practical 24

- Use appropriate units.
- Use decimal and standard form.
- Use an appropriate number of significant figures.

Construct and interpret frequency tables and bar charts.
Put values into an equation.
Translate data between graphical and numerical formats.
Plot two variables from experimental data.

actical 25

Use appropriate units.
Use decimal and standard form.
Use an appropriate number of significant figures.
Construct and interpret frequency tables and bar charts.
Translate data between graphical and numerical formats.
Plot two variables from experimental data.

actical 26

Use appropriate units.
Use decimal and standard form.
Use ratios, fractions and percentages.
Use an appropriate number of significant figures.
Construct and interpret frequency tables and diagrams.
Put values into an equation with appropriate units, e.g. micrometres.
Translate data between graphical and numerical formats.
Plot two variables from experimental data.

actical 27

e maths you need to use will depend on the investigation, but your investigation is likely to include the following.
Use appropriate units.
Use decimal and standard form.
Use ratios, fractions and percentages.
Use an appropriate number of significant figures.
Calculate a mean.
Construct and interpret frequency tables and bar charts.
Understand simple probability.
Understand the principles of sampling as applied to scientific data.
ı might also need to use the following skills.
Select and use a statistical test.
Understand measures of dispersion, including standard deviation and range.
Identify uncertainty in measurements.

ctical 28

Use appropriate units.
Use ratios, fractions and percentages.
Understand the principles of sampling as applied to scientific data.

ctical 30

Use appropriate units.
Use decimal and standard form.
Use ratios, fractions and percentages.

Health and Safety Information

We have attempted to identify all the recognised hazards in the practical activities in this guide. The Activity and Assessment Pack provides suitable warnings about the hazards and suggests appropriate precautions. Teachers an technicians should remember, however, that where there is a hazard, the employer is required to carry out a risk assessment under either the COSHH Regulations or the Management of Health and Safety at Work Regulations. Mc education employers have adopted a range of nationally available publications as model (general) risk assessment and, where such published assessments exist for the activity, our advice is believed to be compatible with them. We have assumed that practical work is carried out in a properly equipped and maintained laboratory and that any fieldwork takes account of the employer's guidelines. In particular, we have assumed that any mains-operated electrical equipment is properly maintained, that students have been shown how to conduct normal laboratory operations (such as heating or handling heavy objects) safely and that good practice is observed when chemicals c living organisms are handled (see below). We have also assumed that classes are sufficiently small and well-behave for a teacher to be able to exercise adequate supervision of the students and that rooms are not so crowded that students' activities pose a danger to their neighbours.

CLEAPSS School Science Service are reviewing but not trialling this text. Following receipt of the CLEAPPS review any such guidance on how to make this resource conform to the above policy will be incorporated and the resource updated.

Important note

Neither Pearson, the authors nor the series editor take responsibility for the safety of any activity. Before doing any practical activity you are legally required to carry out your own risk assessment. In particular, any local ru issued by your employer must be obeyed, regardless of what is recommended in this resource. Where students are required to write their own risk assessments they must always be checked by the teacher and revised, as necessary to cover any issues the students may have overlooked. The teacher should always have the final control as to how t practical is conducted.

Further sources of information: CLEAPSS, www.cleapss.org.uk (includes Secondary Science Laboratory Handbook ar Hazcards)

Printed in Great Britain
by Amazon

64210462R00093